The Recovering Catholic

Joanne H. Meehl

The Recovering Catholic

Personal Journeys of Women Who Left the Church

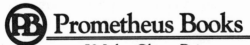 **Prometheus Books**

59 John Glenn Drive
Amherst, NewYork 14228-2197

Published 1995 by Prometheus Books

99 98 97 96 95   5 4 3 2 1

Library of Congress Cataloging-in-Publication Data

Meehl, Joanne H.
   The recovering Catholic : personal journeys of women who left the church / Joanne H. Meehl.
          p.   cm.
   Includes bibliographical references and index.
   ISBN 0-87975-927-5 (alk. paper)
   1. Women, Catholic—Religious life. 2. Ex-church members—Catholic Church—Religious life. 3. Catholic Church—United States—Membership. I. Title.
BX1407.W65M44   1994
282'.082—dc20   94-22774
                                                                         CIP

Printed in the United States of America on acid-free paper.

For my Mom,
who taught me how to be strong,

for my Dad,
who taught me how to be gentle,

for Joe,
who taught me about love,

and for the women in this book,
who taught me about the extraordinary power
of the spiritual.

Contents

7

Preface

For as far back as I can remember, going to mass was a once-a-week event that was saturated in guilt and boredom. The crucifix was above the altar to remind me that Christ died for my terrible sins. The statue of Mary, with her downcast eyes, told me I was too loud and impatient, not meek and mild enough. The words and ritual were impossible to understand. The music was nice, but that was for the choir to sing, not for us in the pews.

I also remember coming out of church, Sunday after Sunday, feeling relieved that I'd done what was expected of me by the church and by my parents, but also feeling wounded, bruised. The only respite from those bleak days began when I was around the age of fourteen; mass held some interest for me those few years because I had become intrigued with boys, and perhaps I would see that cute guy from the next town.

I attended mass during college, initially out of habit and because I lived with a devoutly Catholic roommate, but later because the campus priest was even more vehemently antiwar than the students. Masses were held on campus, and the sermons—actually diatribes against war and our involvement in

11

Vietnam—made the gatherings more protest than religious service, something I needed then. These were the times of Corita's* open and colorful artwork on Catholic church flyers, with brush-stroked quotes drawn from the lesser-known—and thus even more powerful—words of Christ. It was the only time I felt everything was in synch between the church and what Christ said and did. This lasted until the priest was transferred, replaced by a pleasant but bland town priest who did not possess even a spark of the same fire. Now that I look back on these one or two years, they seemed so purposeful, so wonderful, and such an aberration.

My wedding took place in a Catholic church because it was what my parents had wanted, and I figured this was the last time I would have to please them on this count (or so I thought). But from then on, neither my raised-as-Catholic husband nor I went to church, except when we visited my parents—and those old guilt-and-boredom feelings came back every time. After a few years we even declined going with my parents, which disappointed them greatly, although they were not surprised: we'd never had a crucifix in our apartment. We were certifiably "fallen away."

My parents moved south a few years after that, and I saw them once a year or so over the next five or six years.

In the spring of 1984, I visited the Grand Canyon, and for the first time ever, I felt a clear, deep, moving feeling within me that I call *spirituality*. As I sat on the South Rim, being cradled by the canyon's breezes, gulping in the immensity of the place's depths and the supernatural quality of its light, I said aloud to no one but myself, "*This* is where God is."

---

*Corita Kent (1918–1986), for thirty-two years a Sister of the Immaculate Heart of Mary, was an artist best known for her design of the U.S. Postal "Love" stamp.

Thus began an itch that I was able to ignore, for a while, anyway.

When my father died suddenly that August, my grief compelled me to find a reason for his death. In all that pain it gave me peace when I concluded that his dying was a bittersweet signal that said, "I must go back to the church."

Yes, that was it: Go back to the church, because that would have made him happy. Rejoining the church would be poetic in a way, bringing me full circle. I opened my mind and heart to it: I *will* go back to the Catholic church. Probably a lot of the old, recriminating stuff has disappeared, I guessed, and now I would enjoy the liturgy, now that I am more mature, now that I am seeking a deeper meaning. I felt open, yielding.

So I went to the Catholic church in the town where I live in Massachusetts. There I saw so many neighbors that I felt self-conscious. What if I couldn't remember how to genuflect? Other things made me uncomfortable, but I could not sort them out until I went to mass at a church in another town where I did not know anyone.

After three tries, after three headaches, I did not go back. It was because, sadly, nothing had changed. The children were still restless, unable to comprehend the adult dogma they had to listen to; in fact, one time the priest stopped the mass so he could separate two boys who couldn't contain themselves. The priests and the laity, while I was "away," had kept alive all those symbols that long ago made me feel inadequate: the holy water, with which I should bless myself before entering the church so I could wash away any last-minute venial sins; the statue of the Virgin Mary, whose purity I attained only when I was too young to understand what "purity" really was; and of course the crucifix. But the worst were the words, which were still saying, "You are bad, bad, bad. What sins did you commit this week? Did you live up to what Christ expects you to be?"

Why go somewhere every week when it would only make me feel down on myself and especially bad because I'm a *woman*, like Eve, the one who messed it all up?

I also picked up something new: It was the feeling of the place, really of the gathering of the people there. It was the same feeling I'd had when I was seven and nine and fifteen and twenty-one, but only now could I put this disabling ache into words. *The people there exuded both a helplessness and an undercurrent of simmering anger.* As I sat there, I thought it is as if we are all on a subway platform, waiting for the homebound train. The train is late, and we are beginning to shift our feet in impatience. We keep checking our watches, leaning over to look down the tunnel for the oncoming lights. If we had taken the bus home, we'd be there by now. But we've missed the bus, and if we leave the train station now, we'll surely miss the train, and we'll have no way of getting home. Helplessness and anger.

I never went back to either local parish. But I wanted to find a church community, a group of people who felt like me. So I talked to people, asking them for ideas. Then I visited churches, attending services; I felt like I was shopping around, but I knew no other way. Within a few months, I found a church that felt, for the first time ever in a church, like home for me. Upon entering, I saw happy faces. Looking around, I saw symbols that gave me reason to *smile.* During the service, there was a strong sense of exploring, of sharing, of warmth. Members even led parts of the service that they had written themselves! Children had their own understandable service in their own chapel. For the first time ever, I saw that going to church could be a *joyous* experience, one of fellowship and not a guilt-ridden, individual, mandatory task to check off my week's list so I wouldn't go to hell.

I was amazed. I was overjoyed. This was now home for me.

After a few months of attending my new church, I noticed a pattern. When I asked many other women (and men) who visited my new church, "What were you raised as?" they usually answered "Catholic, and I *won't* put my children through what I had to go through!" They, too, had few positive memories. Like me, they did not laugh about how the nuns slapped their hands with yardsticks if they broke a rule; this happened to my mother over and over until she convinced her parents to take her out of the parochial school. (Her crime? She was holding her pen incorrectly.) These women did not chuckle with affection about nuns' warnings to avoid wearing patent leather shoes so that boys could not look into their reflections to see your underwear—something they realized later was so absurd they were embarrassed they had believed it.

I was struck by the anger and defiance—and fear—in these women's voices. I understood exactly what each woman meant.

Why did we leave the Roman Catholic faith? Why won't we raise our children as Catholic? Why do we fail to laugh at "cute" Catholic jokes? Why do we call ourselves "recovering" Catholics? What has made us so angry? And why is that anger still alive after so many years? How did we feel about leaving the fold? Why won't we go back? And how have we changed since then? "What" are we now?

I have written this book to answer those questions, both for myself and for all who have left the Catholic faith, or who are still stuck in "lapsed" status.

What would my father think of all this? He *would* be profoundly sad to know that his first-born is no longer Catholic, no longer part of a religion he dearly loved, with the whole, long-leaving process brought to a climax because of his death.

What I felt at the Grand Canyon and have since carried around with me is a power that I now know is not limited to one glorious place on this earth, but instead is the spirituality within each person.

I am certain that my father would be happy that I have found this joy.

Introduction

Q. VII: How can we prove that the only true Church of Christ
is the Catholic Church?

Answer: We can prove that the only true Church of Christ is
the Catholic Church because . . . the history of the Catholic
Church gives evidence of miraculous strength, permanence, and
unchangeableness, thus showing the world that it is under the
special protection of God.
                            —*The New Baltimore Catechism* (p. 217)

Being a writer means that I am a reader, so my curiosity about
other women who had left the Catholic faith sent me to the library
shelves and data services. When I began to check for existing
literature to learn if other women's reasons for leaving the Catholic
faith were similar to my own, I was stopped short, because there
was no literature, there were no studies. It was as if being an
ex-Catholic was something so impossible to be, that no one had
ever bothered to explore the subject.

I couldn't possibly be alone, but at that moment, that's how
I felt. I simply had to find other voices, other women who felt
like I did, outside of my little Unitarian congregation. So I placed

advertisements in various publications, including the Unitarian Universalist national magazine *The World* ("Woman Writing Book, *Catholic Women: Stories of Anger,* wishes to survey women of all ages, practicing, 'lapsed,' or ex-Catholic"), *Psychology Today* ("Woman Writing Book, *Women Raised Catholic: Stories of Anger,* wishes to survey women, all ages"), *National Catholic Reporter* ("Woman Writing Book, *Women Raised Catholic: Stories of Anger,* wishes to survey women, all ages. Especially interested in how you were treated differently than boys raised Catholic"), and local papers. I asked women "who were angry with the Catholic church" to respond. I used those words because I wanted to survey women like me, those who, prompted by anger, had taken some action to be away from the church.

That small amount of advertising generated 130 responses. The tone of so many of the women's words was "I've been waiting to get this off my chest." I *wasn't* alone!

I sent them all questionnaires, asking them about specific incidents or stories they wanted to tell, about sex and birth control, about guilt and sin, about their spirituality. The questionnaire is at the end of this introduction. Over eighty of the women wrote or taped responses; I interviewed some who were in my vicinity. Much of the material is personal and close to their hearts, and I am grateful for each woman's trust. Each woman chose or was assigned an alias so that I could quote her freely. A key to the women is at the end of this book.

Of the 80 women, 33 are married or remarried, 18 are single, 18 divorced, 2 separated, 3 widowed, and 7 gave no indication of their marital status. Of the 48 women with children, they average about three children each. The women's ages range from 18 to 70, with an average age of 38, and they live in 25 states and the District of Columbia.

Obviously, this is not a scientific sample. Such a sample

would be difficult to obtain: there is no one definition of "ex-Catholic"; indeed, there are those who do not attend mass or receive sacraments yet they consider themselves Catholic.

Along with their writings or their tapes, the women sent other items, such as relevant articles, poems, song lyrics, their own essays, and even a junior high textbook used in the 1950s. I come away impressed by their generous willingness to join me as I explored a subject that still so sharply touches them.

They wrote their stories at their kitchen tables, on looseleaf notebook paper; they used typewriters, dot matrix printers, and tape recorders.

They are office assistants and teachers, programmers and homemakers; they are from "middle America." Only two were ever students of theology. While a few would proudly call themselves "feminist," most do not see themselves as such, despite the feminist thinking they exhibit.

I read stories that moved me, and others that angered me, and occasionally I laughed. I felt a tie with these women. I continue to feel awed and humbled, because the women are articulate yet ordinary, wise and wonderful, and powerfully spiritual.

Their words highlight many of the sections of this book. Other parts draw on my experience working with ex-Catholics who are struggling to give a voice to their new expression of non-Catholic faith.

What is remarkable about the quotes is that these formerly Catholic women, who were raised in diverse parts of the country, over several different decades, say so much of the same thing: They talk about how they grew up in a church that did not—or does not—include them, and about how that exclusion and other related experiences negatively colored so many aspects of their lives.

Some of the energy expressed here is sharp and angry. In

our culture, angry women conjure up ugly, frightening images; some readers may react in fear. But unless anger and frustration are expressed, healing cannot take place. For the women who offered comments included in this book, this catharsis proved to be very therapeutic: they said they could now go forward. Part of their catharsis was knowing they might be helping readers like you.

As I worked with the material I realized it would be most helpful as a guide to other women. If you are a woman who picked up this book, you probably share your reason for reading it with other women. For example, perhaps you have your own children now, and you are getting family pressure to have them "receive the sacraments." You don't want that for your children, yet you *do* want them to have some sort of religious upbringing. Or perhaps you don't go to mass any longer unless it's at Christmas or Easter, and then just to please your parents. Or maybe you simply sense there must be *something* out there for you, some church or faith that could give you spiritual joy. What is said in this book is written to be a help to you.

This book is not for women who wish to stay within the church and change it. Nor is it for those rare few who were not affected by their Catholic upbringing. It is for those women who are considering leaving Roman Catholicism behind, those of you who need to know about others who have felt the way you do. It is for women who want to move on but need encouragement and guidance to do so. It is for women who have given up on a church that has not been home for them, and who refuse to give up on themselves.

Before you begin reading the material, you may want to answer the same survey questions the women in this book did. They are on pages 21-23. What are *your* responses to the questions? After you jot down your answers, you can compare your responses to those of the women. You may have much in common with them.

Except for the occasional addition of necessary clarifications, which are noted in brackets within the quotes, I left the women's words as they were written or spoken, so as not to alter their meaning or change their individual voices.

These were the questions the women answered; I asked them to tell me stories about:

- What prompted you to first start asking questions

- How guilt may have played an excessive role in your experiences with the church

- How you may have been made by the church to feel secondary to men; to your husband, if you are married, rather than as a partner to him; and secondary to children

- How you may have been discouraged from asking questions or from "finding yourself"; how your intelligence may have been underestimated

- If you went to Catholic school, what did you feel about the nuns then, and what about now?

- Did you/do you see any difference in the way boys were affected by their Catholic upbringing? If so, why?

- How the church may have denied your humanness

- How you may have learned that sex is for the greater good of the church and society, not for your own joy and pleasure

- How you may not agree with the church on birth control, abortion, and related issues

- How you were expected to remain a virgin, while boys were merely "discouraged" from sexual activities

- Why you may not want your daughters—and sons—to be brought up as Catholic

- How you have been excluded from playing a more active role in the church (as opposed to men)

- What about the church makes you angriest

- What, if anything, you feel positive about in the church

- What, if anything, would bring you back to the church (if you are "lapsed")

- What you see as the future of the church

- What changes the church must make

- What social and religious options you may have chosen for the rest of your life

- What has been the reaction of your family (parents, siblings, children, husband) to your leaving the church

- Other topics you wish to address?

This was the information about themselves that I asked the women to supply:

- Name
- Alias
- Address/phone
- Age Range

- Marital status
- Children
- Occupation
- Were/are parents Catholic?

1

Questioning: The First Step Out

Q. 204: How can a Catholic best safeguard his faith?

Answer: A Catholic can best safeguard his faith by making frequent acts of faith, by praying for a strong faith, by studying his religion very earnestly, by living a good life, by good reading, by refusing to associate with the enemies of the Church, and by not reading books and papers opposed to the Church and her teaching.

—*The New Baltimore Catechism* (p. 96)

"Why don't you just leave?"

Why the big deal? Why not "just leave," as many non-Catholics suggest to their tormented Catholic friends?

To put such a move in perspective, one has to immerse oneself in the thinking taught to children being raised Catholic. It is difficult for those not raised Catholic to comprehend the enormous power the church holds over the psyches of Catholics, especially women.

Imagine you are a child. You live in a world where your parents and the other grownups tell you that you belong to the only *true* church, the one Christ *himself* founded. Because of that, you are so lucky, and so special. You are also told that any other religion isn't real, and if you attend a service at another church, or if you become friendly with those people, you or your family could suffer in hell (where the pain is like being burned all over with cigarettes), or, almost as bad, you could be converted to their false beliefs.

It is not easy to be a member of the only true church. So, at every mass, for the hundreds of masses you will attend before you graduate from high school, side by side with other children and adults, you renew your vow of belief in your church with something called the Apostles' Creed.

You are told that because you are human and although you are only a little girl, you do bad things called "sins," and you must keep track of those sins so you can confess them only to the priest, who, as God's representative here on earth, can forgive these sins and wipe them away. Because you descend from Eve and because of her sin in the Garden of Eden, you are told that you will suffer tremendous pain during childbirth.

The church's rituals are part of every aspect of your life, from your rising in the morning (morning prayers), to each meal (grace), to each action (Is this a venial sin? mortal sin?), to each thought (the same as an action), to going to sleep at night (night prayers, Act of Contrition*).

---

*A Catholic would say this prayer at bedtime as a way of asking God for forgiveness for that day's sins; doing so could prevent you from going to hell if you die in your sleep. The Act of Contrition: "Oh my God, I am heartily sorry for having offended thee, and I detest all my sins, because of thy just punishments, but most of all because they offend thee, my God, who art all-good and deserving of all my love. I firmly resolve, with the help of thy grace, to sin no more and to avoid the near occasions of sin."

The grownups teach you that you must raise your children in this same religion if you want to be a good church member and an admired Catholic woman, whose role is to make sure her own family is Catholic. And, when you grow up, if things don't go the way you'd thought they would, you learn that you must stick it out, and suffer; this pain is part of the suffering that those in your church, especially the women, must endure to gain God's grace. After all, Christ died for you. You can endure a little suffering, then, too.

Then imagine: despite this cocoon of security, you have questions. Some things don't fit together, some are not helpful, and some even seem to contradict each other. You're puzzled and curious. This scares you. So you raise your questions with a priest, the adult who is your bridge between here and Heaven, but he views your questions as a challenge to their authority, and as evidence that you have doubts about Christ's word. No, you say, it's not that at all; I just want to know.

Dismissing your query, the priest pats you on the head. Your family frowns at you for the trouble you're causing, wondering aloud if "enemies of the church" have influenced you. A nun may snap a retort like one did to Susan, 42, who today is a psychologist in Michigan: "Who are you, with your little mind, to question the great minds of the great men of the church?"

Everyone seems to get upset. So, you swallow your questions. It just isn't worth it. You can't seem to find anyone who can answer them, and that nice priest who used to explain the gospel during the children's mass was transferred to another church over the summer. So you'll just hope that your questions will go away. And you'll try harder and harder to understand those things you don't understand, praying to God to make you a good enough person to accept what you don't understand. If at first the prayers don't work, you'll pray even more fervently. You'll go to retreats and novenas;* maybe they'll stamp out these thoughts that could weaken your unquestioning acceptance.

Simmering Doubts: "The Catholic Loop"

Nothing really stamps out the questions. Instead, they simmer, only to resurface later, often coupled with a healthy dose of frustration or anger. As a woman, you now have problems that are *not* helped by what you learned in church. Reality is not as they'd pictured it for you. Or you now have your own little girl, and you can't answer her questions about God with statements that don't make any sense to you.

To begin to have questions, even doubts, about the Catholic church—this institution that is so much a part of your life— is a frightening thing. And to pursue these questions and doubts is a brave step because it means stepping back and objectively viewing the only church you have ever known, a church that has woven its way into every part of your life and the life of the family who loved—and loves—you.

The unhappy Catholic travels in "the Catholic Loop." This is a circular path that always brings one back to the same place. When someone considers exploring religious and spiritual options outside the Catholic church, obstacles usually arise: often they involve family expectations, and the fear of being rejected. Then again, it could be a concern over some sacrament: "What will happen if I die without the last rites? I'd better just stay here." Then there is fear of the unknown outside "the church, the only

---

*A novena is a concentrated series of prayers said over a nine-day period, usually done for a special favor or purpose, such as solving a health problem for someone in the family.

true church." Such imbedded teachings are powerful, as is the guilt they inspire when a Catholic questions the church. To question is to disobey.

So the unhappy Catholic has only two choices: stay in the Loop and put up a good front in order to keep family problems, guilt, and fear at bay at the cost of personal unhappiness; or just stop going to church, and do nothing else—no searching for happiness in another church, nor renunciation, perhaps even no thinking. It is making a decision without making a decision. It is the safest option; it is less upsetting than the unknown of being outside, or stuck inside on the Catholic Loop, painfully trying to fit the impossible mold of being a "good Catholic." This is the state of being "lapsed" or "fallen away." Catholics caught in the Loop are in a true limbo, neither in or out.

Objectively viewing the ubiquitous familiarity of a psychological (and spiritual) construct—the institution and beliefs of the Roman Catholic church—is the first step in the act of leaving it behind. This chapter addresses the fears about having such thoughts, such questions; here you are allowed to experience those doubts, to have your questions.

What *were* your first questions about the fallibility of the church; what *are* they? I call them "prompter" questions because they prompted the women you'll meet here to think about going elsewhere for the answers. Maybe you, too, have thought of looking for answers beyond the church heirarchy.

By disclosing what provoked them to ask these questions, these women show us how hard it is to pick the lock of Catholicism. For those of you who are troubled by the questions and concerns that appear to shake your faith off of its foundation, these women can empathize with your frustration. You're not alone. You are one of many who probably haven't had anyone to talk to.

Sin and Guilt

Some questions are prompted by fatigue over what might be called "soul bookkeeping," or the warehousing—at least until the next confession—of sins, and the tracking of indulgences and graces. The young Catholic learns categories and earns credits, but she is like Yosarian in *Catch-22*, always having to do one more thing to gain purity of soul and personal goodness. Falling short of that, she remains a flawed human being, forever striving to do more and more to earn God's love and forgiveness. So the church defines the disease—being a sinful, guilty, imperfect human being—and promises the only available cure, Catholic forgiveness.

This constant vigilance creates guilt, which resonates in the words of the women quoted here, and is discussed in chapter 2 as a main reason for their decision to leave the Catholic church. When they first realized that they could never be good enough, many of these women began questioning their allegiance to the church.

Dealing with real life as young adults pushed the women even further away from Catholicism. Jill, 30, a counselor in New Jersey, "began to ask questions when it became more and more difficult to be human. Everything was rated as sins, and what would happen if you committed such a sin." Janet, 45, of Vermont, says that when her first baby was being baptized, "I heard words like 'the sin of Adam and Eve,' and 'devil,' and other words, that sin was in my baby. How can you say this baby is sinful? You're crazy!" Later, when she used birth control pills and felt guilty, she "began to feel irritated that the church could have such control over people's lives," and began to withdraw. "Once you start questioning one thing, you have to question it all."

Katrina says, "If we were created in God's image, then God

must be both male *and* female." If the church hierarchy were to read this book, I hope they see that women are the strength of the church. (Indeed, on Sunday mornings, most churches' attendance is dominated by women.) When women leave Catholicism, the church not only loses its heart but its brains and brawn, for it is the women—those who do so much of the church's work—who are looking for new churches where they can freely give their energy at every level. Perhaps the old men of the church will see these women, in Colorado and Louisiana and South Dakota and elsewhere throughout the country, as they see themselves: in Paul's words (to the Galatians 3:28), as "neither male nor female: for ye are all one in Christ Jesus."

Birth Control, Abortion, and Real Life

The irritation—some would say fury—with the church over birth control is shared by many women raised Catholic. I remember my own mother, to this day a devout Catholic, saying more than once, "If the priests want me to have lots of children [she wanted three but had two], let *them* buy their bottles, their diapers, their clothes, and their college educations!"

"When I was pregnant with my ninth child," says Peggy, now a fifty-nine-year-old widowed homemaker in South Dakota, "I went to confession to a visiting Benedictine monk—not my parish priest. My husband's health was deteriorating and I was upset about this new pregnancy. Instead of the usual 'This child is God's will,' he listened, thought a long time, and then said, 'You shouldn't be having all these babies.' I thought a clap of thunder had entered the confessional! I couldn't be hearing right! A priest telling me there was another way? I came out of there, a forty-year-old woman, with my mind opened to a new way of living—formation of my own conscience, not waiting for a priest, pope, or bishop to tell me what to do next. I was an authority on my own life!" The monk gave Peggy consent not to get permission any longer, thereby freeing her. Ironically, it was a man of the church who gave Peggy license to question the men of the church. Sadly, some women need this permission, so deep was their indoctrination in the tenet "do not question."

For Cyndy, a twenty-six-year-old teacher from Pennsylvania, real life conflicted with church teachings in a very personal way during her senior year in high school: her fifteen-year-old sister came to her for help in getting an abortion. "I paid for her abortion," despite the films she and her classmates at Catholic school had to watch of abortions and fetal remains. "I had been taught that anyone who has, helps, pays for, or even allows an abortion is excommunicated immediately from the church. I didn't leave, not yet. But the straws were adding up."

Kathleen, 36, is a single mother who lives in Ohio. Her husband left her during her pregnancy with their child, a first baby they both had planned and waited for. He then divorced her, against her wishes. She realized what would happen if she raised her daughter within the Catholic church: "My daughter will be taught that I'm a sinner if I marry my boyfriend because he also is divorced. Aha, the old Catholic church catch-22—we 'gotcha' labeled a sinner no matter what you do!"

For some, the questioning came later. "It was only after I was married that I started to question the right of a priest to sit in judgment of me," says Kelly, now a forty-five-year-old officer worker from Illinois who is married with four children. "Once I started to really look at it, it all fell apart in front of my eyes. The priests and nuns started leaving their orders in record numbers and I knew that the whole thing stunk." Indeed, why *were* "God's representatives on earth" leaving the fold? And why are they so difficult to recruit today?

The Nature of God

As girls, some of the earliest questions were prompted by confusion about the nature of God. Is God loving, as was being taught by the nuns and priests, or is God vindictive and an angry spy-in-the-sky, as was also taught?

Polly, 30, of Massachusetts, describes this as "the dichotomy between 'God the Redeemer' and 'God the Vengeful.' . . . God was watching and might even strike me dead if I sinned too much," which contradicted another teaching that said, "God would never do anything to hurt those who loved him." When Polly was a teenager, her nineteen-year-old sister-in-law died of cancer, and Polly's brother was left to raise a two-year-old son. "I decided that the God I had been raised to believe in—the all-good, all-loving God—couldn't possibly exist . . . and I wasn't struck dead. What a revelation!"

Irene "didn't understand how a God such as the one we were taught to love and pray to, could be so cruel and angry as to have created a hell where those who commit one mortal sin would burn forever, or a purgatory or limbo for those unlucky enough not to have been born Catholic." Along those lines, Victoria, 57, a teacher in New York State, wondered why, as she had been taught, one could go to hell for eating meat on Fridays, and one could go to hell for murdering someone: "Obviously, these two things were not equal in weight," yet the punishment was the same. "Eventually at one Sunday mass when I was a teenager I wondered if going to mass, receiving communion, all the ritual, and confession meant *anything.* From that moment it never meant anything again."

Being away at college, of course, causes many young people to question many areas of their lives. Ironically, it was Martha's studies to become a nun that drove her out of the church. Now thirty-five and a staff assistant in Massachusetts, she was in her first year at the convent when she began "to address the real issues of my distorted belief system as a Catholic woman. Ironically, it was in required classes that I first 'saw the light.' Suddenly my understanding of scripture was being transformed by modern biblical scholarship."

Obeying the Ruling Elite

Not being able to become an altar boy, or altar server, prompted many questions from the women when they were girls. Regardless of how they feel about the church as adults, the women interviewed said that not being allowed to become altar children was a profound and hurtful revelation about their church. Martha said, "For years I watched boys dressed in junior-sized cassocks and surplices, with grass-stained sneakers peeking out from beneath, mumbling their lines. Looking at the Latin text in my mother's missal, I knew I could do better. I also knew better than to ask to try."

Anita is thirty-eight, a writer, nanny, and divorced mother of two who lives in the Boston area. She was at an all-girl, all-nun retreat when a priest came to say mass, and they needed an altar server. She was thrilled to be chosen. Then, at the priest's side, "as I watched him hold up the host for all to adore as Christ, I looked at the rows of young girls and nuns with their attention fixed on the priest. That was when it hit me, that 'connectedness' of the priest with God that the nuns could never have. At that moment, I wanted to be a priest." When she went home and declared her intention, "I was ridiculed. It was just something that couldn't be done" because she was a girl. For such a young person to be so sensitive to the power of that moment only highlights the losses the Catholic church has suffered by excluding women from the priesthood.

Hypocrisy within the ruling hierarchy caused questions. Annmarie, 21, a student in New York, witnessed political clashes in her Catholic high school administration over a sports program: "I saw un-Christian—never mind un-Catholic—behavior" on all sides in the situation, "so I really started asking questions." Lola lives in Virginia, where she is a hair stylist. She is thirty-five, married with no children. Lola's parents had priests to the house for dinner. "They drank a lot, and smoked, and talked about other people. It just didn't fit with what I had been taught about priests, nuns, and the church. I guess that's when I really started questioning the church." Connie first started asking questions when she was in Catholic nursing school. "The nuns were so un-Christlike to each other I couldn't imagine why they were nuns." Jimi's divorced mother was ignored and virtually shunned at her church, which spurred Jimi, now thirty-eight and a single library clerk in California, to "question not only the Catholic church but also this 'God' I had been taught to believe in."

Catholics are taught that theirs is the only true church. But adherents to other faiths seem devoted to their churches, and happy with them, which prompted Kaye of California to wonder: They "were not given a complete identity and brain-washing. They seemed to go to church for Bible lessons or for joy rather than to avoid sin."

Darla is a forty-nine-year-old travel agent in California who is married with three children. She and her husband "met people who practiced birth control and they were nice people. I met people who didn't go to church—they were nice people. . . . If I broke loose of the bonds around me, would I become a sinful, despicable person? Could I actually think and choose and come out good? Hurrah, the answer is yes. . . . I like myself better, I like the world better, but the church is something I cannot abide!"

Most of the women who have left the church do not laugh when someone talks about patent leather shoe jokes or corporal punishment by nuns or priests. Their memories are too bitter. When Nicole's parents could not afford the altar boy dues any longer, "the priest would not accept my brother's excuses . . . and he became very irate, slapping my brother across the face . . . , resulting in a tooth literally being knocked out of his mouth!" This incident "sparked an internal rage, but because I was trained to respect all clergy, my rage was suppressed." Later, this same priest, training the ten-year-olds for the traditional confirmation ceremony "tap" on the cheek from the bishop, "would swing out his arm and slap us. He used force. . . . The boys were sometimes sent reeling . . . another boy had a tooth injury. The priest remarked that the boy was not strong enough yet." The irony was that this confirmation incident left Nicole questioning rather than solidifying her faith in God. She is forty as she recalls this story she remembers so vividly.

Diane remembers when she was eight or nine years old and her family could not go to a wedding at a Protestant church, something then banned by the Catholic church. She asked her parents, "Why can't we go? If we're the best and we're the chosen, why can't we go? What are they afraid of?" Today she is a forty-six-year-old company controller in North Carolina who does not go to any church.

Many questions were raised by the changes prompted by

Vatican II in the 1960s, the all-church conference called together by Pope John XXIII, considered one of the most progressive popes in church history. While many of the changes were implemented to strengthen the Roman church, they also prompted an unexpected exodus. Renegade priests still do Latin masses, because of their deep meaning to so many pre-Vatican II Catholics; others disliked changes such as those in nuns' habits. Helen, now a forty-year-old homemaker in Arizona with one child, says such symbolic changes caused her to question deeper issues: "All of a sudden it was OK to eat meat on Fridays. If it was so easy to change that which had been a sin, then how important were any of the other rules, and why should I believe in them?" The church had become trapped by their own rules, their attempts to control the flock.

Glenna is fifty-one. She is a married fiscal coordinator from Pennsylvania with four children. She first had doubts during Vatican II, but for very different reasons. "My break with the Roman Catholic church came after forty years of blind obedience to laws that I now know were man-made, not God-made as I was told throughout my life by the hierarchy of a religion that I finally see to be, at best, anachronistic; and at worst, a threat to society." During Pope John XXIII's tenure, Glenna realized "the infallibility of these people in matters of faith and morals was invented by the Catholic clergy. . . . I will always remember this stage of my life—my early thirties—as the beginning of my separation from the church. It also marked the emergence of my anger and resentment, as I realized how completely my life had been controlled by the lies and manufactured dogma of men who neither knew nor cared about the human suffering for which they were responsible."

Unsatisfying Answers: "It's a Mystery" and "You Must Obey"

Do you remember what was said to you when you asked a question the adults in church could not answer? "It's a mystery." So many Catholics, the women here included, remember this response.

"It's a mystery" was interpreted by girls to mean, "God knows all, we cannot even attempt to know as much, so don't ask." Later, when we were maturing young women, it was interpreted as, "We don't know, so stop asking."

But the questioning came anyway. And the church moved quickly to squelch it. This was done in a variety of ways that silenced the girls, and later, the young women, but it did not eliminate the uncertainty.

To questions such as "Where was the justice in a child being killed by a car?" and "Why are some people so rich and others so poor?" Irene, 35, a divorced payroll clerk in California, received answers such as "God knows why and you must have faith and not question such an all-merciful, powerful God who works in mysterious ways." When Kaye asked questions at her Catholic high school about birth control, she was told, "You are guilty of pride. Your disagreement is based on sin, an emotional flaw, . . . sexual urges and lust. Any more questioning of matters of faith and morals' was forbidden" or she would lose her high school scholarship. Apparently the church itself did not work in such mysterious ways.

Jennifer never revealed her inquiring mind. "That would have been dangerous. It was safer to try to swallow the answers in the *Baltimore Catechism* (which I did) and to repress the self as much as possible. Questions were discouraged, and questions on religion were forbidden. It was expected that we believe what we were told and—unfortunately—most of us did." Today Jennifer is a forty-five-year-old writer, married, who lives in Missouri, and is a Unitarian Universalist.

Martha recalls "warnings from the pulpit . . . scolding us for acts of faithlessness. . . . Don't forget Doubting Thomas, or Zechariah, father of John the Baptist, who was struck dumb for questioning God about how he and his wife could bring forth a child at their advanced ages. All creation had been accomplished ages before we had ever appeared on the earth, so who were we to question the work of the Lord, not to mention two thousand years of tradition? Our job was to obey, like the 'soldiers of Christ' we became at confirmation."

Kelly received the usual "it's a mystery" answer, along with, "You must have faith." Those answers "covered almost every question you could ever ask." Later, she swung the other way and became a skeptic, questioning everything. "I swear I will never be so totally fooled again. . . . I accepted everything they told me. I believed it all. Everything. What was not to believe? Mom believed it. Everyone in school believed it. Most of the neighbors were Catholic. What's not to believe? So I was almost twenty-seven when I really started to wake up. I never went back."

Sara says the church "can't let people intellectualize or know too much or no one would stay. . . . A strict Catholic upbringing dwarfs people intellectually by using brainwashing techniques and intimidation. The church is as bad this way as the Moonies." Paula was told that she would never find the answer "so stop asking. I was asking my questions, not 'theirs.' I think because Catholicism is so conforming, it stagnates you." Today Sara is forty-one, an IRS clerk from Texas, divorced with three children.

Asking questions *is* dangerous, as Jennifer said. "When that

Catholic egg began to crack," says Dottie of California, "it *cracked*. The whole thing is suspect. Now that I am beginning to look at it . . . I marvel at my forty-year captivity . . . with never a whimper!"

Is it any wonder you've pushed away your doubts, your questions? After years of obedience training, mostly done during your vulnerable and impressionable childhood, it *is* difficult to acknowledge your disagreements with what you've been taught by the one true church. The cocoon you were taught would take care of you has unraveled. If the first recognition of this was stark enough for these women to remember it, you probably do, too. It marked the beginning of the end of being a good Catholic girl.

You wouldn't know where to begin in knitting a new cocoon for yourself, and it *is* easier to tuck the loose ends in where they can't be seen. You've probably been doing that: you've swallowed your questions and doubts, and you've become "lapsed" or "fallen away," which is really a no-decision decision. If that non-decision feels all right to you, you don't need to read any further. But if it gnaws at you, as it has with the women here, check their reasons for leaving the "lapsed" status. Some of them may be yours.

2

Guilt, Sin, and Shame for Being Human

Q. 60: What are the chief punishments of Adam which we inherit through original sin?

Answer: The chief punishments of Adam which we inherit through original sin are: death, suffering, ignorance, and a strong inclination to sin.

Q. 387: How can we make a good examination of conscience?

Answer: We can make a good examination of conscience by calling to mind the commandments of God and of the Church, and the particular duties of our state of life, and by asking ourselves how we may have sinned with regard to them.
—*The New Baltimore Catechism* (pp. 31, 169)

The reasons why women leave the Catholic church are not always specific or related to a key, identifiable incident, though there certainly are stories that would fit this category. More often, the reasons are based on deep feelings not tied to one event but then—and even now—are entangled with self-concept.

Put another way, you probably have picked up this book not because of any specific incident, but because of some vague resentment or negative feeling that won't go away.

I am often asked, usually by people with a knowing tone in their voices, "Women leave the Catholic church because of the abortion issue, right?"

If that were true, there would be one-third fewer women in Catholic churches, because Catholic women, as a group, obtain abortions in the same (and some say, greater) proportion as other American women. While disagreement with the hierarchy about sex, birth control, and abortion may be the straw that breaks the camel's back (see chapter 4), the deeper reason why women stop going to Catholic church is that it makes them feel negative about themselves, both as human beings and as women. They seem to feel as strongly about this as "abuse" as they would about incest, for example.

In this chapter, and in the next three chapters, I let the women's words speak for themselves. They need little or no comment. My intention is that you will come away from reading these chapters saying, "I wasn't the only little girl who went through all this. And it isn't just me who feels the way I do now."

Denied a Childhood

Many of us who are no longer Catholic do not think of our childhood churchgoing days as happy. Instead, as most of the women quoted in this chapter say, we spent our childhoods wondering if we were properly keeping track of our sins, hoping we would remember them correctly for confession, and hoping we'd remember them all.

Cathy is a thirty-five-year-old homemaker from Colorado, and married with two children. She recalls that, "A friend of mine once asked me, 'Do you know the difference between Jewish guilt and Catholic guilt? The Jews receive their guilt from their mothers; Catholics receive their guilt from *everything!*' "

She adds: "The guilt I experienced in my childhood was incredible. I feel denied a childhood due to my preoccupation with sinning and [obtaining] a priest's forgiveness. My anger here lies with the church condemning children for normal behavior—our venial sins of sibling fighting, anger with parents, and 'impure' thoughts!" Her words encapsulate the women's resentment toward the church for its condemnation of normal behavior.

Susan, the psychologist from Michigan who is married with two children, says that if one follows the church's thinking, "It's a sin to be a child. Part of being a child is getting in touch with your 'primitive' feelings, to live out fantasies, to not clean your room. But all of these are sins according to the church so everything that's small-child-like is a sin. So just *being* for very much of Catholicism is a sin. . . . To base this whole economic and structural system [the church] on what is a lie [list of sins] is very dangerous, and very cruel."

"The church concentrates so much on the negative," says Katrina, 40, a divorced mother of one and traffic clerk in Illinois. "Seems like I always felt guilty about something! And going to confession every week meant trying to dredge up all the bad things I did that week, or making some up to have something to say in confession. . . . The church seldom seems to teach the positive side of the message Christ brought." No wonder so many of the women say they have problems with their self-esteem: each week they had to remember their flaws.

Jimi, the library clerk from California, asserts, "Confession is supposed to help you with guilt. But I think it just keeps a person under the church's thumb. I think the doctrine of original sin [that you are born sinful] is very harmful and leads to a lot of abuse."

Jill believes that, "Because . . . everything was so guilt-oriented, there was no room to make mistakes. Being the awkward, imperfect child that I was, there were always times to be self-conscious and sorry for things that I had not even done. I was far from perfect in many areas, but shone in others although the good sides of me never materialized until later. I . . . hated myself and became a rebellious teenager who became suicidal.

"Finding myself was difficult because it was always conditioned. The imaginary 'rule book' was present—always consciously thwarting spontaneity. Anything that concerned taboos such as sex, drugs, alcohol, or weaknesses were unacceptable. In terms of intelligence, precocious children were not smiled at. Independent thinking or exploration was discouraged, and in my case [that made it] more appealing." One wonders if she chose her occupation of counselor to help herself become a more questioning and independent thinker.

Janet of Vermont recalls, "We were machines, marching silently, two by two. We bowed our heads. We didn't speak unless spoken to, and we spent long hours in church on our knees. We examined our consciences ad nauseum. We kept trying and trying to find things that we had done that were bad that we could confess. . . ."

Jennifer of Missouri says it still makes her angry: "I was so victimized when I didn't have the capacity to protect myself. I was simply too little to resist, and was brainwashed terribly. I am angry that I was so sucked in. That I spent so many years trying to be an impossible something held up to me as the goal."

Georgia, a direct-mail specialist, "never—even from the earliest days—felt a closeness for my religion. I felt since I was born into it I had no choice in the matter and—as a catch-22 situation—I couldn't get out of it, either, without guilt and sin. That is, I couldn't practice my religion in my heart, but I couldn't *not* practice it without fear of retribution from family and God." Because her mother invoked God's name whenever she disciplined her, Georgia "soon saw God as a punishing, critical image. I knew, just as I could never please my mother, I hadn't a chance of ever making it to heaven. . . . Just being a normal seven-year-old—the age of reason when you become responsible for your soul—entailed a lot of daily venial sins which were impossible to avoid but which had to be confessed in order to receive communion and *that* was required every Sunday." Today Georgia, 44, is separated with one child.

Natalie, 31, a married homemaker in Massachusetts with three children, remembers the day she made her first confession: the monsignor became angry with her for not following the correct format, even hauling her out of the confessional in front of family and friends. "I lost my dignity and trust that day to a person who was never taught the simplest lesson in life—to be kind."

Martha addresses the church-humanness question another way. "Do I have to love Jesus?" she asks. Then she answers as she remembers she would have as a little girl. "I'm afraid of him. He yelled at his apostles a lot, because they were always doing something wrong. He expected them to know things they never had a chance to learn. Supposedly he loved the children, but I don't trust him—he never seemed to smile or laugh. He died for my sins, but I'm only a kid and I'm trying so hard to be good so my parents and other people will love me. Does he expect I'll never be good enough? I feel guilty for resenting his death. I never asked him to die for me, but I'm supposed to be grateful."

And she asks, "Why is it when I do something right, it's

because God gave me the grace and strength to do it; and when I do something wrong, it's because I'm a weak and sinful creature? Can't I take credit for the good stuff? I don't blame the devil when I'm bad." Martha's question is important: it goes to the heart of the church's condemnation of things human.

As a woman, Martha asks, "If not only words and deeds but *thoughts* can be sins, what am I supposed to do . . . put a lock on my brain? Go to confession every five minutes? What if a car runs over me right after I've thought about the Mother of God being a boring pushover, and I die in a state of sin?"

Jennifer says, "My memories of communion time at Mass were of painful moments of feeling unworthy in every possible way." She goes on to say, " 'Finding oneself' was a foreign concept. 'Oneself' was inferior to the Almighty God. Serving God was presented as the only thing worth spit. The best way to serve God, the nuns insisted, was to negate the self, to do penance, to suffer. Becoming selfless was the ideal." And, "I was taught that humans were always dangerously close to damnation. That only by striving beyond the frailties of humanity was salvation to be achieved. The divinity of Jesus was stressed far more than his humanity. (Today I pretty much hate Jesus. I regard him sort of as the big brother that got all the goodies and was Mom's favorite. Perhaps I'll get over this; I rather hope so). The 'Holy Family,' with its wimpish Virgin Mother, its poor Joseph (the stepfather who never counted for much), and its divine son who always had an incredible edge on the rest of us, was held up as the perfect example of what families should be. I looked at my own family, so human and frail and gathering around the table for dinner each night, and knew there was no way to be saved.

"I tried to picture the Holy Family sitting down at my dinner table for burgers and fries. I began to feel as though I could not be human and religious at the same time, and tried to suppress my humanity at every turn. The abyss between religion and my everyday activities became wider and wider, and were soon separated by a partition of unreality. . . . I soon began to feel that I could never be good enough, pure enough, strong enough, to make it to heaven."

Bernice, a married mother of one and a writer in her 40s who lives in Connecticut, remembers being taught, "We should not pray directly to God because we are unworthy human beings. We need a mediator and that is Mary. We should pray to Mary who will wrap our puny prayers in a golden halo and present them to God for us." This writer remembers night prayers to a favorite saint, asking the saint to talk to Jesus for her so that she herself would not bother him.

And those prayers themselves helped strengthen the notion of inherent evil and weakness, Kaye notes. "We were drilled in such prayers as the Hail Holy Queen, which gives a self-description of humans as 'poor, banished children of Eve, we send up our sighs, mourning and weeping in this valley of tears . . . , after this our exile. . . .' What are humans but exiles in misery with no hope but salvation? We are sinners."

One of the women says, "The church attempts to instill a sense of sin in every Catholic individual—even children as young as five years old—in catechism classes. The emphasis is on why you're born evil, how you sin daily, and how, if you don't confess and repent, you'll never go to heaven or be worthy of God. Making mistakes is part of being human, and yet, the church cannot and will not accept it. What could a five- or six-year-old possibly have done that was so wrong? It is criminal . . . to mold a child to believe he is inherently evil. It stifles spontaneity, creativity, self-esteem, trust, and love for one's self, as well as creates a fear of God." Speaking is Anne, 20, single and a student in New

York. She was one of the youngest respondents to the questionnaire; judging from her comments, allegations that "the church has changed" are not true.

Many of the other women had similar things to say about the church's treatment of children, allegedly the church's most precious asset. Cathy of Colorado says, "Children are truly a gift and the Catholic church denies their humanness. Generally, as children, they are 'sinning' constantly. How good can you feel about yourself when you are constantly confessing (such as 'thinking a dirty word')? Young children's energy, teenagers' questioning, and adult anger are all disallowed. Our sexuality is disallowed ('Pray that those thoughts go away'). I would challenge any priest to show me the Catholic church's unconditional condon[ing] of any human act."

Kelly, the mother of four in Illinois, was four when she started kindergarten because her birthday wasn't until December. "Pretty young to be such a 'bad girl.' I learned from Sister Elaine right away what happens to bad little girls who don't do what they are told. I think it was a homework assignment that quite a few of us hadn't turned in. We had to stand in line and watch as each one of us was struck across the back of the hand with a yardstick. What a painful, humiliating thing for a little four-year-old girl. Why do I feel like crying for that little lost me?"

Nora, 44, is single with one child and lives in California. She says, "I've learned to cry for my inner child who never really got to be a child, and the teenager who came out into a world totally different from the convent life of the nuns who taught me."

In Catholic grade school, Jennifer adds, "Hell was pictured as never far away. The sisters told us stories of otherwise good little children who slipped [into sin] once and were run over by cars and went straight to hell. Or little girls who got angry with their parents and left the house in the morning without saying goodbye and then Mommy got killed and the little girl felt horrible. Stories like these were standard fare during religion class." Jennifer was not alone: this writer remembers a priest asking us children to "imagine your mother dead, in her open casket on the altar, her sweet face in peace, and imagine how you'd feel if you've been a bad little boy or girl. Now think of how much better you'll feel if you're a good little boy or girl." I did not attend Catholic schools; I like to say I was traumatized enough on Sundays alone.

Susan, the psychologist, maintains that, "Guilt does not change behavior. It just causes neurosis. The church is a pathological system. . . . The bureaucracy, hierarchy, and patriarchy [of the Catholic church] are all based on something that's not true; that God can hear you, listen to you, and change things, is not true at all. . . . In an alcoholic family, it's wrong to *be*, to think, to want, to do any of those things . . . and all those things are a sin [according to the church]. . . . The Catholic church is analogous to an alcoholic family system in that it is a church of guilt and shame. It's a shame-based religion. . . . They use guilt and shame to control people."

Damage: "The Claws of Catholicism"

Janet puts it graphically: "It took me thirteen years to get what I call 'the claws of Catholicism' out of my back, until I felt free of that thing that hangs over your head and pushes you down."

One woman remembers being scolded, along with another girl, by the parish priest for "something I did during mass that caught Sister's attention. . . . I was being judged. . . . We were sinners, no two ways about it. We started sinning our first day of school and we just piled sin upon sin. The heartbreak of my story is that I know now that I was a nice little girl and I am a great person. But buried deep inside is the knowledge that I'm bad. How many times can you be told you're bad without something inside believing them?" I call this phenomenon "Catholic shrapnel"—the damage of thinking of yourself as "bad" goes deep, causes grave injury, and takes a lifetime to work itself out, if ever.

Myra adds, looking back on other damage, "I believe that I and many Catholics became alcoholic because the drug helps to cover up feelings of guilt for the time [being], helps you be something you aren't supposed to be." Myra is fifty-two, divorced with five children, and is a registered nurse in California.

"A negative loop was begun in my mind," says Carmen of Alaska, "which, looking at it now, seems every bit as evil as witchcraft. I feel that the church's main reason in doing this as a matter of course with programming, ritual, and many other ways, is to never allow the person to feel his/her own natural connection to . . . whatever you personally call God. . . . Inside I thought everything was a sin, had no self-confidence of any sort, and began an inner dialog with myself which constantly spun around in my mind all the time, and if . . . I would have any normal feelings for my age, I would usually confess it as a sin (just to be safe)."

Judy, 48, mother of five and an office supervisor in Colorado, recalls, "God was presented as a Santa Claus who saw all and knew all. You can't get away with anything, not even your thoughts. As a young child I felt guilty about everything. I was always sure that I'd forgotten something [in confession] or was afraid that I wasn't really sorry and would go to hell anyway."

Victoria says, "The church I grew up with just picked at you all the time. . . . I felt guilt for having liverwurst on Friday, for normal (or abnormal) sexual feelings. . . . The priest yelled at women for wearing too much makeup, at people [in general] for not giving enough money. . . . I took it seriously: I worried about brushing my teeth Sunday mornings—would it be breaking the fast before receiving communion?" And like many of the women who talk about confession, she "added a lie" instead of confessing another act, or she made up sins so she'd have something to say in the confessional.

"Boy, my whole life has been a series of guilt trips," offers Connie. She is sixty-three, a married registered nurse in Florida with two grown children. "I was raised in Catholic schools, nursing school, and as an adult—age fifty-nine—graduated from a Catholic college, yet I felt I never did anything right."

Adele "regularly felt guilty *for the class* when a nun would bawl us out for disobedience, even when I'd been silent and behaved perfectly. It was not until much later in life that I read about 'corporate guilt,' and realized I'd been hard on myself." Adele is a twenty-five-year-old college student advisor from Nebraska and single.

"When one goes through life feeling guilty about everything, it's hard to feel good about yourself," says Sara. "Guilt was used to break my spirit, bruise my ego, and make me into a pliable puppet. I was never taught to behave out of respect for myself and others. Nor was love used as a reason to be good. It was always guilt mixed with fear. . . . I finally ended up in therapy for five years to correct the damage."

Loretta is a divorced, forty-eight-year-old mother of two and a computer systems analyst in New Hampshire. She says, "Shame is something I deal with to this day. For me, it's rooted in the many years of being told (or at least hearing) that I was an unworthy being, and that if I tried very hard, and for the rest of my life, I just might have a shot at becoming a decent enough person to make it into 'heaven.' . . ." When she was about ten or eleven, Loretta was "kneeling before a huge crucifix in the church . . . feeling so ashamed because it was Lent, and the nun had been repeatedly reminding us that we should try to *feel* the passion of Jesus carrying that cross up to Calvary . . . that he carried it because of my sins as well as everyone else's. I remember feeling guilty because I didn't think I *really* felt the sadness as much as I should. I practiced and practiced, and I finally succeeded at internalizing sadness. I carry that sadness around at some level to this very day! Knowing how sick that is and being aware of it aren't enough. I must constantly remind myself that *I do not have to be sad.*"

Rosalie, 31, salesperson and divorced mother of one from Oklahoma, thanks the nuns for making her sensitive to others. But she later realized that they carried a good thing too far: "Until very recently, I consistently put others' wants, needs, and desires ahead of my own. I believe the source of this was the 'deny yourself' indoctrination I received in those daily catechism classes. For years and years I have been saying, 'I'm sorry,' 'Excuse me,' 'Pardon me' when other people stepped on *my* feet or bumped into *me*. Once again, I think the source is the 'Be humble,' 'You are not as important as others' lectures I received daily as a child."

Janet maintains, "Just by calling it the 'Holy Mother Church' implies guilt, because mothers inspire guilt. Guilt was a big issue. People were kept in line with guilt." Without this power to effect obedience from its followers, the church would lose members, and thus lose clout.

Kelly says, "The only way to beat this [Catholic] system, I decided, was to do everything I could to make them happy. Forty years later I am still trying to make everyone happy so that no one will think I'm a bad girl."

In Kelly's case, as seen with others, the damage was also

to others in her family: "I don't blame the church for all of this—most of it came from my mother. But where did *she* get it? She went to the same school that I did, a parish of lower-class Irish blue-collar workers. She tried to exorcise her demons by reliving her school years through me and my sister. . . . She constantly tried to incur . . . the nuns' favor. I must have carried a thousand cakes she baked for them over to the convent. The message she gave me was that the Catholic church was absolutely the most important thing in our lives. She was deeply immersed in it. Never question anything a nun tells you, we were told. The nun . . . is the Bride of Christ."

As she was growing up, Cathy, like other children, went to her mother for advice. "If I asked any personal questions, she directed me to a priest, a nun, or prayer for the answer. I never knew her—she denied her sexuality ('impure'), her femininity ('vanity'), and her humanness ('sinful'). The church was her 'out.' She didn't have to take responsibility for anything in her life—she made no choices—she followed the church. She never questioned. . . . I hate the church for absolving her of her parental/womanly responsibilities. What I mean is that she *was* the church."

"Even now the anger that preceded my separation from the church lies just beneath the surface," Glenna says. "This is probably due in part to the fact that my mother, the daughter of old-country Italian immigrants, is living out her 'golden' years in a state of depression that I believe was caused by suppressed anger over her treatment at the hands of the church. Unlike me, she never did break away. She still attends mass regularly, still fights a daily battle with inner guilt and conflict that was nurtured for years by an uncaring religion."

Many of the women left Catholicism with other remnants of childhood lessons. When Phyllis, a thirty-nine-year-old restaurateur from Ohio, takes her mother to church, "I can feel myself tighten up when walking through the door. I refuse to kneel down, so I sit in those parts of the mass. My body language the whole time is very telling; my arms are crossed and I can't wait to get out of there. . . . My anger is based on how many years of thinking and learning I lost. We were literally brainwashed and taught not to think or to question. How very stupid."

Roberta's account states, "It has taken me years of struggle, psychotherapy, education, reading, and thought to get over the problems and hangups my Catholic upbringing caused. I wonder if I will ever be over it." She is in her thirties and lives in New York.

"The thing that makes me the angriest," Kelly declared, "is the thought that I might have been a better, different, more self-assured person if I hadn't been subjected to the shame, guilt, and humiliation they dealt out to me for twelve years. That's a long, long time to be held hostage and not be able to use your head."

According to Jennifer, "By the time I got to college, . . . I had lost the ability to be introspective, to doubt, or to question. I was emotionally very fragile, and religiously, I was a wreck. I struggled throughout my college years, making the honor roll and becoming more obsessive-compulsive as I went along. I was anorexic in college, losing fifty pounds one summer by starving myself. I know [now] I was trying to get control of myself somehow. The controls being imposed on me at church and at home were intense. So I was trying to match that control inside myself. . . .

"When I was twenty-one and a senior in college, I suffered an emotional collapse. If I were to put a label on what I was suffering, I would say I was a very fearful obsessive-compulsive.

"My parents sent me to our Catholic M.D. He referred me

to a Catholic psychiatrist, who, after one visit, committed me to a Catholic psychiatric ward. He diagnosed me—incorrectly, I found out years later—as a paranoid schizophrenic, and began a regimen of anti-psychotic drugs that was to continue for more than ten years. While I was hospitalized, my doctor forbade me to go to mass, so it was apparent even to him that the church was tied up in my illness.

"Over the next six years, there were three such hospitalizations. I cannot blame the church entirely for my psychiatric history. But certainly a large part of the responsibility lies like a bundle of dirty laundry at the church's door. . . .

"It took years of therapy to retrain me to look inside myself and to question anything. I had become almost robotic in my acceptance of fate and in my belief that I was unable to control my own life.

"God had quickly formed in my mind as a hit man who was out to get me. As an adult in therapy, I have struggled to undo many of these 'little girl truths' that took shape in the early Catholic grade-school classroom. Not all of them, certainly, were created by the church. Given the predispositions of my personality and the vagaries of my home life, the guilt-inducing properties of my church became lethal emotionally. . . .

"During the last ten years, good and gentle therapists have helped me undo much of the religious damage of the first twenty-five years of my life. They have proven to me that the initial diagnosis was a tragic mistake, and that I am a strong, healthy woman with much to offer.

"One of the legacies of my Catholic upbringing is phobias. I am currently in therapy with a psychologist who specializes in their treatment. He is, remarkably, a Unitarian like me. He says that a large percentage of his patients are Catholics, former Catholics, or members of other strongly authoritarian religious groups."

Others would agree with Jennifer, who says, "I believe that the church either promotes obsessive-compulsive behavior or perhaps that is just the way I reacted to it as a teenager, but I tried to be perfect . . . and it carried over into many aspects of my life. The good thing is that I do try, but the bad things about behavior like this are many, and it ties a person up by trying to control or think he/she has control over certain variables . . . that we have no control over. . . .

"I also see that the time I spent being a Catholic almost drove me insane, and I have been consciously undoing their programming ever since."

Some of the women have had extensive therapy to remedy the earlier damage. Susan "spent over $10,000 just this year [1987] on therapy trying to resolve the abuse I received in a 'good Catholic home.' Bondage, enemas, sodomy, and torture coexisted with daily mass and communion, Tuesday night novenas, Thursday night Holy Hours, Saturday confessions, and, of course, Sunday services.

"I'm pissed at my parents; I'm pissed at the priests who heard their confessions; and I'm pissed at a do-nothing church. . . .

"I'm pissed at Mary, my only hope, my thread of sanity, for being an ineffectual role model. And I'm pissed at the God who sent the answer of 'No' to a sexually abused three-year-old, four-year-old, five-year-old, six-year-old, seven-year-old, etc. . . . The irony of it all was that after eigtheen years of abuse, I was still a virgin! Can you imagine? Anything and everything else was done to every orifice but the 'sacred one.'

"My father was raised in a seminary, so he was probably abused himself. I know at least one brother was abused—my mother was into enemas."

Bernice, the writer in Connecticut, found that real life conflicted with childhood teachings. "When economic necessity forced me to get a . . . job [outside the home], I was filled with guilt. Though my income was absolutely necessary to keep us off welfare, I always felt I was depriving my husband and son. I felt I was a failure because I did not live up to the expectations drummed into my head by the nuns [to be at home]. It was many years before I started to believe in myself enough to know that the choice was mine: to work inside the home or not, and that I did not have to feel guilty."

Katrina is resentful that, "The Catholic church taught me *not* to think—and it's taken me a long time to even realize that! I never question authority—the sisters sure drummed *that* into me! And I find now that I realize that I resent the *hell* out of training that taught me to turn off my mind instead of turning it *on*—just shut up and be a 'good' girl!" She adds, "Seems like you couldn't do anything without having to feel bad about feeling good!"

Irene adds, "Much too much emphasis was placed on discipline in a negative fashion. I have never developed very much self-esteem because praise [both at home and at church] was nonexistent and blame was all too evident." She says she found herself in a pattern of searching "for another man. I can look back on all this and I still don't know how to break this mold. I feel stuck by my desire for love and my lack of self-esteem. My mother still doesn't understand why I don't practice 'my faith' and continues to try to make me feel guilty." Irene says she has broken away but, "What I did not realize at the time was that my subconscious was carrying all those Catholic lessons . . . and they continue to influence me."

Patricia says she is "not really bitter about my Catholic childhood. But I'm glad I've left it behind as much as I can. I am conscious of how my attitudes, especially my low self-esteem, are due in part to my Catholic childhood."

Another woman commenting on her lack of self-esteem is Loretta of New Hampshire. "I am now forty-eight. I spend a lot of energy trying to work on my self-esteem. One of the outcomes of my [Catholic] indoctrination was a deeply embedded belief that I have no worth. This self-esteem issue is the number-one problem in my life today."

She goes on to address the subject of Catholic jokes, those stories that make light of nuns using yardsticks on children. "Several years ago, I went to see a play called *Do Patent Leather Shoes Really Shine Up?* As the audience around me laughed uproariously at what was being said, I simply could not see the humor in it. I was over forty at the time. Shortly thereafter, I bought a couple of joke books that contained similar material. The same thing [occurred]. I had long before stopped attending mass and had recognized my extreme anger at the church, but until that moment, I had not truly realized the extent to which my Catholic indoctrination had affected my life. Even today, after having dealt with that part of my history in therapy, I still cannot always see humor in Catholic jokes." Kelly of Illinois says virtually the same thing: "My sister and I were talking about her trip to see the play *Nunsense*. She saw nothing funny about it. We had the same reaction upon viewing *Patent Leather Shoes*." Susan saw *Nunsense* and sensed anger around her, people who really didn't find the material funny.

Susan attributes problems at home and her Catholic girlhood with teaching her "how to watch people very early—[I] learned how to be, how to behave." Reacting to all of that now, she says " 'Fuck you' has become a theme in my life. I saw the film *Hail Mary* and I loved crossing the picket line [of Catholics protesting the movie]!"

Barbara of Texas, 43, is married with two children. She sees that her church upbringing "set up an abuse pattern" in her life:

"a wimp/passive pattern that I was stuck in," thus allowing her first husband to abuse her. "The church played a role in my staying so long with him" because of church prohibitions against divorce. She left anyway, and says, "ironically, God—not the church—helped me through" that tough time. Also, "other people, non-Catholics, who were *nice*, good people, helped me be more positive, [and] make something of myself."

As Darla, the travel agent and mother of three, says, "The Catholic church had created such tight bonds to keep you under their control, we lost the freedom to think and grow up. The church kept us forever children, obedient out of fear, which they tried to convince us was love." Perhaps, by not "allowing" children to be children, the church creates dependent, childlike adults.

Cathy looks back at her " 'good Catholic girl' image and how committed I was to it. It has run my life—the guilt, low self-esteem, and paranoia that has followed me all these years brings to mind the little girl in church, kneeling up straight, chapel veil on her head, hands perfectly folded, praying for forgiveness for what I *might* do wrong."

"No one can hand us a religious blueprint for living and expect complete obedience," notes Kelly. "I was controlled and manipulated and finally taught to defer to almost everyone. I have been fighting the effects of this religious upbringing ever since."

Tina, a thirty-eight-year-old caretaker in New York, admits that, "Despite having an M.A. degree in philosophy, I plod through life afraid of my own shadow. When will a nun pop out of a stairwell, accusations running wild? 'Stand up straight,' 'Don't talk,' 'Keep in line.' " She adds, bitterly, to the end of her type-written response to the survey, "Please forgive the lack of perfect typing and grammar. As a graduate of a Catholic high school, I am never to turn out a piece of work that is not perfect in every way. Please let no nuns read this, as I fear being kept after school."

Sexual confusion was a long-lasting effect of Catholic upbringing for some of the women, such as Loretta: "If I ever had strong urges and desires, . . . I certainly buried them deep enough so that they stayed repressed for many years. Any hint of sexual feelings left me with feelings of great shame."

Carmen feels the same. "I denied myself pleasure in many ways, and even after I was married I had to continually fight consciously to be able to enjoy sexual pleasure. . . . It wasn't that I believed that sex was a duty really, since I thought husband and wife would be allowed to enjoy themselves *after* marriage, but I denied so many physical feelings, I barely knew which ones were natural feelings of pleasure and were to be enjoyed, and where discipline was involved."

Others agree. Sara admits: "I still have some problems today. At the age of forty-one, I have never experienced a climax with a man. I think this is directly connected with the sexual attitudes the church and my mother taught me." And Margot, 41, an administrator and married mother of two in Vermont, adds, "Until I went into therapy at thirty years of age with two ex-nuns as therapists, I was stuck in the 'good girl, don't think' syndrome. I had 'man' issues. The nuns had me deal with a male therapist who'd been a seminarian. I got rid of my anger, guilt, and old way of thinking through this. Until then priests had been on a pedestal. I got to know them as people. It was mind-boggling to learn they were as screwed up as the rest of us."

Abby, in her late thirties, summarizes: "Anything human was considered bad: sexuality, feelings like anger, etc. It's not surprising that Catholics have to spend a lot of time later in their lives putting themselves back together, considering we have to deny all these parts of ourselves that are normal and human."

Today she is a psychologist in New Hampshire, married with one child.

Forgotten Land Mines

Susan refers to what I call the "forgotten land mines" of Catholicism. When the nuns at her high school realized she would not go into the convent as they had wanted her to, and she would instead go to a state university, and perhaps get married and have a family, they told her, "If you don't follow your vocation [to become a nun], you'll never be happy, you'll have an unhappy marriage, you'll have a terrible time." Susan says, "Those words came back to haunt me when I was in labor with my first child. I wasn't doing what they wanted and now I'm being punished."

Others talk about their forgotten land mines. Glenna notes, "When I least expect it, I get a twinge of the old fear." Helen of Arizona had sex before marriage and, "I still believe deep down that I'm going to pay for the premarital sex."

Coping Through Duplicity

Maggie acknowledges that she "eventually learned the 'confess but don't tell all' method of other Catholics [in confession], and continued to be one for a while, but on the birth control pill. This was a time when people went to confession in one parish where the priest 'allowed' birth control and to communion at their own if their priest didn't! . . . If anyone overheard my obligatory Christmas Eve confession [one year], they (and the priest) must have thought they'd found a sure-nuff saint! My first lesson in religious hypocrisy." Maggie is fifty-six, a married homemaker and mother of four children, who lives in South Dakota. This coping through duplicity that she describes is a phenomenon familiar to those raised Catholic: if their parish priest won't let a couple write their own wedding vows, they'll go to a priest two towns over that they've heard about through the grapevine who *will* allow it at his church. Or if someone has had an abortion and wants a confession without being excommunicated, Father So-and-So at St. John's will hear your confession, *and will understand and forgive.* Or there's the former nun who will help you tell your children about methods of birth control. It is as if there is this underground church that the people themselves have created, filling in the blanks with the people of the traditional church who *will* help them.

Dusty, 36, a divorced mother of two from Pennsylvania who is an editor, remembers, "My mother would tell me what to say in confession. Once, she caught me masturbating. She told me to tell the priest that I touched myself in bad places. I was eight. I thought this was really stupid. I couldn't believe it was a sin. I figured my mother had gotten something wrong. So instead of telling the priest (and dying of embarrassment—you couldn't tell me they didn't recognize your voice!), I did this: I added on one more 'disobeyed my parents,' and one more 'lied.' I figured that way I was covered. So when I got home from confession and my mother asked, 'Did you tell the priest what I told you to tell him?' I could say yes. That was the 'lie.' The 'disobey' was the part where I didn't do what she said." One can marvel at such exquisite reasoning by a young child who had learned "the rules" she needed to follow in order to be a good Catholic.

More than a few Catholics used this cover-all-the-bases method. Linda, a twenty-year-old student from Texas, remembers how she "lied in confession, made up sins, sometimes told the truth. Either way it made me feel bad. To say so many Our

Fathers and Hail Marys felt like a punishment to me. I was unable to see that as a cleansing of the soul."

Geraldine, a widow and teacher who at "around seventy" was the oldest woman to answer the questionnaire, argues that there is a "brought up Catholic" personality: " 'Save the surface and you save all' is instinctive almost for those of us brought up Catholic. You learn early to beat the system, to hide from and deceive the watchful nuns and priests." She adds cynically, "We make good bureaucrats, politicians, and public relations specialists."

Suffering and Pain Are Good

Rosalie of Oklahoma "can remember lying in bed in the darkness of my room pinching myself until I was black and blue just to offer up the pain for Christ because He died for us. I remember hoping my pain would make Him feel better." Later: "Then something worse than physical pain became a part of my life when I was six: the mental anguish that I suffered when my parents announced that they were going to be divorced. It became my responsibility to save them both from eternal damnation which I hoped I could accomplish by gaining indulgences for them earned through my reciting Hail Marys and Our Fathers." Kaye, also, "tried to save all of my family from hell by praying for indulgences. More than one priest had told me I'd have to choose between going to heaven by myself or to hell with those parents of mine" who did not attend church.

"My sexual fantasy life is very masochistic," Cyndy of Pennsylvania notes. "I fault the Catholic church and its guilt-driven, sex-is-bad, you-will-be-punished mentality; i.e., since I'm not allowed to enjoy sex, yet I do (immensely), then I must be punished for it. . . . I remember reading . . . about the saints (those wonderful saints whom I should try to live my life like) who constantly whipped themselves, slept on beds of rocks and sticks, wore thorned belts under their clothes, and generally tried to hurt themselves and suffer as much as possible. . . . And I was rewarded by the nuns for reading the stories of torture! The message was clear: abuse your body and suffer, and good will come out of it."

Elaine, in her forties and a divorced shop owner and mother of three, remembers "with horror the tortured pictures of saints [which] were everywhere." Each church seemed to try to outdo the next with paintings of bloodied martyrs.

Ginny is a nun of fifty-eight who answered the survey. I include her in the book, although she is still a nun, because she tells us what is was like—and is like—to be a woman of the church (especially in the next chapter), yet she sees herself as *apart* from the church because of the changes she has made in her life. Ginny wore her habit and participated in daily mass and other services until she took a sabbatical to obtain her master's degree. She says her studies caused her to question everything about her role as a woman, a nun, and a person within the Catholic church. She returned to her religious community radicalized; she no longer wears her habit, does not attend daily mass with her sisters, and relishes her faith in her own way.

Ginny remembers that as a new nun, "we were to beat our sinful bodies into subjection. A whole new list of sins was now added to my previous list. Looking at oneself in a mirror or daring to glance at one's body while bathing, desiring to wear a bra or girdle, allowing hair to show from under the veil [and the like] were all terrible sins. . . . For most of my life I was so overwhelmed by guilt that on three different occasions I was hospitalized for depression. Because it had been so ingrained in me that I was a bad person and no decent man would want to marry me, I entered religious life to make reparation for the terrible sins *I* 'committed' between the ages of five and eleven when my brother sexually molested me."

The Wild Side: Mother Teresa versus Joan Collins

Tina says, "I was raised to be Mother Teresa, but I long to be Joan Collins [who played Alexis Carrington on television's 'Dynasty']." She is not alone.

Myra says, "I rebelled in my thirties. I did everything that I wasn't supposed to. I had affairs, had 'fun,' was married and divorced twice—I went all out. . . ."

Evelyn, 29, says she "became an outlaw," and was "an artist in Haight-Ashbury for the latter part of the 1960s . . . LSD, free love, a lot of idealism, which of course, had to die. My poor, poor nuns would have stroked out." Today Evelyn is a married homemaker in South Dakota with one child.

Terry, 33, makes an observation similar to the one that says kids who go to Catholic schools have the best dirty jokes: "I've noticed that many of the Catholic school girls I knew from the neighborhood where I grew up went from being very prudish in school to being extremely sexually active after graduation. I remember the public school girls to have been more middle of the road and centered about their sexual development." She is now a married nurse who lives in Connecticut.

The Recovering Catholic

Adele, Abby, and Loretta, among others, refer to themselves as "recovering Catholics."

Linda of Texas declares, "In AA for a long time I've said, 'My name is Linda and I'm a recovering alcoholic. I'm also a recovering Catholic. . . .' I'm not the only recovering Catholic in AA. I've had the opportunity to attend meetings all over the city of Houston . . . , all over the state of Texas and everywhere else I've been—San Francisco, New Jersey, Oklahoma, Florida, West Germany, and just about everywhere else in between. I also know a lot of other . . . alcoholic and nonalcoholic recovering Catholics. So I know I am not alone and not unique."

Kaye says, "When I first left the church I faced all the fears of eternal damnation and superstitions about punishment. . . . I don't feel that now."

A Therapist's View

Kathleen Rooney, MSW, is a clinical social worker/therapist with Versacare Outpatient in Attleboro, Massachusetts, an agency whose specialty is recovery services for drug and alcohol abusers. Raised Catholic herself, and having rejected the religion, Ms. Rooney validates much of what the women have said here about the damage Catholicism has done to them. Some of her recovering clients are women (and men) who struggle with what they were taught and how to change thinking which has compounded or even lead to their drug or drinking problems.

She says, "So many things about the church teachings take years or even a lifetime to get past. There's always that feeling of 'they're gonna get me.' The scars it leaves include guilt; and the feeling that even though you're doing what's right for you, you're *bad*, and God is an angry man who will be angry with you. Also, one is often left with the feeling that unless you're perfect, you might as well just give up—perfection is the only goal. And, if you suffer, on some level you must deserve it for *something* you've done." She adds that the paternal, patriarchal system focuses not on how members treat one another, not on *dos*, but rather on being "overly controlling of personal behavior" (sex) and on the *don'ts*. "They pay lip service to how we treat one another. Jesus would be appalled at this self-perpetuating bureaucracy." To illustrate her last comment, she points out the difference between how Pope John Paul II "speaks out of both sides of his mouth: in Poland, he wants the church involved in the new government, but in Mexico, where the church has more to gain by lack of involvement, he has ordered a lack of involvement."

She adds that when women are battered, they come away thinking "somehow it's their own fault. Their church upbringing has taught them to stay in the marriage no matter what."

What about sexual abuse by priests, which has rocked many a community in recent years? Rooney answers, "It is inconceivable that the church hierarchy did not know about this. What kind of message does that send to children? That it's more important to protect the church's appearance than it is to protect children."

As if to underscore this point, a news story in late December 1993 described how the Catholic archbishop in Hartford, Connecticut, "overruled a plan to open a soup kitchen because they thought it would hurt the church's image . . . that a downtown soup kitchen would harm development, affect the parish's image negatively, and strain what the archdiocese called the parish's 'shaky' financial prospects" (*Boston Globe*, December 29, 1993). The howl of protest by local residents and other clergy over this decision was enough to ruin their image on its own. It is these kinds of acts that continue to fortify the opposite image: that the Roman Catholic church is a business more interested in keeping itself going than in doing the work Christ founded it to do. Jesus, indeed, would have been appalled.

3

Women, Less Equal Than Men

[We say] men, not women, because Christ did not make even
His own Mother, or the angels, priests.
—*The New Baltimore Catechism* (p. 192)

The rejection of women priests goes deeper than the hierarchy's
defense of an all-male priesthood based on the teaching that Christ
chose only male disciples. The women here, since childhood, have
perceived an official condescension toward women, despite some
parishes' need (due to shortages of men) for women lectors and
eucharistic ministers. The women address this "secondariness"
in this chapter.

"You're Just a Girl"

The women were asked if they perceived any differences between how Catholic boys and Catholic girls were raised. Their
responses are tempered by the fact that their religion, especially
before the 1970s, was couched in a culture that largely ignored

or objectified women. But some things still stand out as distinctly Catholic in influence.

According to Janet, "Boys, and men, seem more able to laugh about it [being raised Catholic]. . . . It doesn't seem to have injured them . . . like it did the girls. They were altar boys, the privileged ones anyway."

Ronnie, 23, a therapist in California, summarizes: "The patriarchal attitude gave boys a sense of entitlement." Barbara of Texas remembers she was told by a nun that "a boy is worth more than a girl, a boy is worth three girls," an arbitrary ratio that obviously stuck with Barbara for decades.

Susan remembers, "You're just a girl" was a constant theme. "Boys went up for communion first, into church first. . . . Boys didn't listen [to the nuns] or didn't believe them, therefore they survived. . . . [The message was that] women are inherently evil seductresses."

Several of the women had other comments on boys being raised Catholic. "Right from the beginning, it seemed that the boys were given special attention," asserts Debbie, a thirty-six-year-old divorced mother and military administrator in Washington state. "As soon as my brothers were about ten years old they were allowed to miss church, etc., because they were boys," adds Holly, a thirty-nine-year-old married mother of two and educational consultant in Colorado. Connie, 63, remembers: "Boys were always allowed more leeway in my generation, and Catholic upbringing was no different. They were always excused for their behavior."

Sara remembers the boys who went to the Catholic boys' school: "They seemed more sure of themselves, weren't quite as intimidated as the girls, and also didn't seem to have understanding of the girls' feelings. In a way they seemed a bit cold emotionally and all the ones I met felt the man was the boss. The church breeds misogynists."

"Overall I think boys grow up feeling that they have more power in the church, and they do," observes Jimi. "But they can be very warped by it."

The church hierarchy maintains that women have a special role within the church, and defines it as one that is considered sacred: that of being a mother and/or a servant. Chris of Pennsylvania, who at eighteen is the youngest respondent to the questionnaire, remarks scornfully on that "special" role as servant. "When I was . . . in Sunday school, the priest came around the building, asking for volunteers to be altar boys. I thought it would be nice to help out during the church service, so I volunteered, not realizing that altar *boys* were what he wanted. I thought that boys and girls can be firepersons and mailpersons, so why can't I be an altar person? But all I got was a pat on the head and I got sent back to my seat.

"Boys are always superior to girls in the church. Despite what I have been told, nuns are not as important to the church as priests, and I think that it would be very degrading to be a nun now that I have seen the way they are treated. . . .

"Women are supposed to be quiet, naive, nameless people who are only good for having children."

Some of Ginny's remarks are reflections of her years as a nun within the church; other comments tell us what she saw as a girl while being raised Catholic. "Boys and men were allowed to get angry, but girls and women were not. . . . Boys could be altar boys and then priests. In our parish, only boys and men were allowed inside the sanctuary. My dad was janitor and did much of the work in the sanctuary. We were never allowed to help him because it would have been a sin for us to go inside the communion rail. (There was one exception. At Christmas time we were allowed—permission given by the pastor—to help him put the manger crib up and the icicles on the tree.) Several

women were assigned to do the altar linens, albs, and surplices,*
etc., but they, too, were not allowed to go into the sanctuary.
They worked in the sacristy.† Women were also responsible for
keeping the *body of the church* clean—washing walls, benches,
windows, dusting, [and the like]. Dad did the floors though
because of the heavy lifting. Women were not to do heavy lifting,
because they were to bear children and might damage their
internal organs. And that, too, would be very sinful because our
chief role in life was to bring children into the world."

"Of course I was expected to remain a virgin until marriage,"
Adrianne, 24, a teaching assistant in Texas, remembers. "This
matter was never even discussed with my brothers." Another
woman who remembers the same home situation says, "My
brothers had not been expected to be virgins—I was."

This family reinforcement of a church teaching occurred in
another way, as recalled by Adele of Nebraska: "My dad looked
proudly around the table at his seven daughters and three sons.
He used words like 'beautiful' (stressing looks) and 'pure' (stressing virginity and more!) to describe the girls. Once, he even said
he wished all seven of us girls would become nuns. I took that
to mean we would only be clean as long as we were isolated
from men, who would inevitably soil us. I don't think he said
much about the boys being priests, or celibate either."

In Victoria's Italian culture "boys were made much of. The
boys had a specially built high school. They could be priests.
Boys were mysterious and wonderful, and the church reinforced

---

*Albs and surplices are part of the vestments (garments) that priests
wear while saying mass.

†The sacristy is a room just off the altar, where the priest dresses
in his vestments.

this. I wanted to be a boy, a much more interesting thing to me to be than a girl."

But not all the women remember boys being treated better than the girls. Jill says, "Boys were treated just as bad or worse than girls." Another curtly adds her opinion: "I didn't feel any discrimination between the sexes—I felt we were all . . . beings to be brainwashed."

A few even thought that boys were left socially disadvantaged. According to MaryAnn, in her forties, a divorced mother of three, and a teacher in Missouri, "The boys and priests seemed very unhappy and inhibited generally, and definitely immature and not able to develop relationships, but what else is new? The priests, if vibrant, were discouraged by the power structure from caring too much."

It's All Eve's Fault: The Shame in Being Female

"Adam didn't eat the apple. It was Eve's fault. She seduced him into it," contends Terry, about what she was taught.

One of my own memories is learning in Sunday school that because of Eve's sin in tempting Adam, women were cursed forever with pain while giving birth.

Kelly's freshman text in high school told her, " 'A Marylike girl or woman should consider herself blessed if permitted to sweep, dust, and scrub the house of God.' I do remember vividly the three reasons for marriage as taught to me by the good nuns: (1) to have children, (2) to ensure a place in heaven for you and your husband, and (3) to quiet concupiscence. What, I wondered, was concupiscence?" (Concupiscence is defined as "strong or abnormal appetite, especially sexual." Perhaps it is the belief of the church that marriage eliminates sexual desire?)

Loretta remembers "I did find the church to be very male-oriented and did always feel like a 'lesser' being. I believed very strongly deep down, however, that men *were* superior. God, after all, was male. Men were more intelligent. Men had 'something' built in when they were born that made them smarter, braver, more capable, stronger, more astute, and closer to God. That's why God, the pope, and priests were male."

As a girl, Ricki, 32, a married graduate student in Illinois, "questioned more and more what seemed to be the church's expectation of me . . . to be 'a good girl.' This meant accepting the church's teachings and following its authoritarian lead. I increasingly found myself in losing positions; I wanted to find out more about myself and found that, if I continued to follow several of the church's teachings, then I had to deny aspects I was learning about myself, which I was increasingly unwilling to do. That is essentially when I decided to leave the church."

Maggie: "Who do I blame for the way women are treated the world over? That super-patriarchal church that is the model for all the others. You can't debate whether women have souls without someone doubting it. Have they ever doubted whether men have souls?"

"Why are women evil?" asks Holly. "Heck, I didn't know one thing about sex but *I* was considered evil. How can the church claim that *Eve caused* something called 'original sin'? I don't believe that we are born with any *evil* in us, and it makes me angry that women are held responsible for *all* of it."

Martha resents the church's "refusal to recognize the validity of my voice [as a woman] and the quality of my judgment. Like the song says, 'Bless the beasts and the children, 'cause in this world they have no voice, they have no choice.' With neither voice nor choice, one is reduced to a state of perpetual childhood, utterly and forever dependent on the goodwill of one's guardians. Some blessing!"

"When I became a nun," Ginny observes, "my education about women and the church *really* began. First there was a very definite hierarchy: [from the top] God, priests, angels and saints, men who were not clergy, lay women, sisters (nuns), devils. First and foremost, we were to strive to be nonpersons."

Ginny says, "[Like Mary] we were to be humble, obedient, quiet, prayerful, and suffer as she did (suffer in silence—Mary never complained or cried, did she?). And most of all, she took care of Jesus, the High Priest. So it was an integral part of my religious community's apostolate to take care of priests. This meant many things: cleaning their rooms, making their beds, being their maids, serving them meals, taking care of their clothes (mending, laundering, sewing their vestments), polishing their shoes, running all kinds of errands, being their secretary or girl Friday, [and so on]. And occasionally it even meant submitting to sexual favors." One priest repeatedly forced her to masturbate him, then told her she should confess *her* sin. "Damn! Talk about double standards. It was still a sin to get angry, but I would get *very angry* anyway when I would see him say mass in the morning. But I would have to pretend I was sick and walk out before communion since I couldn't receive the Eucharist. I (the woman) had committed a mortal sin. And when I went to confession, *I* had not only committed a sexual sin, but *I* had led astray a 'Man of God.' Consistent with what I had been taught from age eleven on, it was always the woman's fault. Never mind his harassment, his threats. I was even refused absolution on one occasion." This makes for a nice system for the perpetrator— you molest the woman, but you make sure you teach her it's *her* fault; that way you get away with it. Ginny continues, "Speak about anger, hurt, frustration, guilt! Is it any wonder I was hospitalized for depression for five weeks?"

Ginny is angered: "That we have to tolerate a man like Pope John Paul II, Cardinals Law and O'Connor, Cardinal Ratzinger; that our bishops are so fearful of speaking out; the church's treatment of women who wish to take a role in political life or in positions where they could bring about systemic change. I'm angered that so many women have been duped into believing they must be submissive, humble, obedient, and [be] servants to men. . . . I'm angered when I'm reprimanded for using nonsexist language in prayers, or when I refer to God as 'Mother' or 'She.' "

Lily, in her fifties, is a legal administrator in Missouri. She is divorced with four children. She remembers when women, shortly after giving birth, were required by the church to participate in "purification ceremonies" for the mothers. By equating birth with something dirty, the church's action represents, to her, "The theft of honor from women for creating the race," and she relates this type of ceremony to "baptism of infants, ritual-promulgated expectations of 'obedience' to men . . . , all-male priesthood, all-male control of sacraments." She alleges that Cardinal Spellman of New York had two nuns working full-time on his stamp collection. "Perhaps the worst [aspect] is the smug arrogance with which they present their ignorance as the immutable truth."

Reacting to what she was taught about Eve and menstruation, Helen notes, "My greatest anger . . . is at a God who would decide that since the first woman made a mistake that all other women would also have to pay for it every month for most of their lives until the end of the world. How am I supposed to find comfort with someone who did that to me and to all other women? Am I supposed to think a Being who singled out women for pain and degradation really loves and cares about me?" Telling people such tales, then, can backfire, resulting in the creation of nonbelievers.

Some messages are more subtle. Wanda is a eucharistic minister, a lay position considered within the church to be higher status than lector at the pulpit, or altar boy; in truth, they are substitute priests who distribute communion at parishes that need priests. At Wanda's parish, the head priest, after consecrating the communion, serves it to the male eucharistic ministers, lectors, and altar boys before he serves the women eucharistic ministers. He always gives them their communion last. "It makes me angry, but what can I do?" Wanda asks. She is in her sixties and says many parishioners tell her they line up for her rather than the priest because she gives them the communion with reverence, he [gives it] with boredom.

"I'm disturbed that women are oppressed by the church," remarks one of the women. "Our church refused to consider the possibility of altar girls. Girls were for May crowning, that's it. Baptism didn't take away the original sin of being born a female. Women just didn't count. Sex was for making priests and nuns for the future. God invented menstruation to punish women for making Adam eat that apple. Women screwed it up for everyone—how could we ever hope to be loved equally by a patriarchal god and his son? It took me so long to realize that these ideas weren't truths, but were Catholic beliefs which I didn't have to accept. I didn't want to be a helpmate—I want to be a full and valuable person on my own."

MaryAnn of Missouri suggests that "the lopsided view of sin as primarily sexual, and avoiding confrontation of greed, anger, et cetera, was used to keep women down and [it served] . . . the male power structure. I was caught in a web of never-ending self-examination, in which every thought and feeling was questioned, denied, and repressed as 'evil.' "

Anne, the student in New York, believes "Catholic boys, excluding those who are becoming clergy members, seem to be less affected by the stringent tenets of Catholicism. I believe this is due to the fact that the church implies that women are ethically bound to observe the laws of the church moreso than men due to their [the women's] 'evil' nature, and 'inferior' intellectual potential. Also, the church has more laws against women (i.e., abortion and birth control) than it does regarding men."

Candy, a thirty-six-year-old military officer, agrees, maintaining, "The Catholic church to this day insists on forcing women into the background. I mean, women are even told it's against the church doctrine to control their own reproductive systems. When I was a child, only boys could assist the priests; the girls were expected to sing in the choir, and otherwise keep their mouths shut."

"Why are there more women in church than men?" wonders Martha, who studied to be a nun. "I thought men were obligated to attend mass, too. It's a mortal sin if you miss mass, right? Does this mean that all the fathers and husbands who aren't here will go to hell unless they confess this sin?"

Chris alleges, "The church does its best to make women feel like they belong barefoot and pregnant. . . . The men who thought of this must have been very insecure and narrow-minded. Any [woman] who accepts that [she] should take second place to a man must have very low self-esteem. Just because a woman is capable of bearing children doesn't mean that's all she is good enough to do. Men produce the sperm which is half of what makes a child in the first place, yet nobody expects them to be constantly barefoot and reproductive!"

Kaye remembered having "won all the honors in [Catholic] school, but the highest award was granted and then *withdrawn from me* because 'a boy should have it.' "

Susan "had to get the bishop's permission to take chemistry in high school—the nuns wouldn't let me. I wanted to be a nurse. . . . My last master's degree was a 'fuck you' degree. I did it to say to the nuns and hierarchy, 'I can get all As at a top school [University of Michigan], I'm smart enough,' especially after they told me I'd never make it." Today Susan admits that this behavior only feeds into the "good girl" mentality nurtured by the church, and she vows not to play into it again.

Bernice remembers being taught lessons that included: "The purpose of college for a woman: to give her a few years between high school and marriage. The main role of a woman was to be a wife and mother. The man is the head of the house, the woman the heart. A woman is subject to her husband. In an argument, the woman must always defer to her husband's wishes.

"The right place for a married woman is the home. Raising a family is a career blessed by God. There is no need for a woman to work outside the home with the following exceptions: nurses and teachers.

"Though marriage is a sacred institution, the highest calling is to the service of God. Blessed is the mother who encourages her son to become a priest; her daughter to become a nun.

"I left St. John's University after two years to become a wife. The nuns had told us that college was a good place to find an educated husband and earn our 'Mrs.' I entered married life filled with misconceptions fed through the Catholic Family Life program at my church. My role was to be a wife and a mother. Any job I would hold was to be temporary until that blessed day when I became pregnant.

"This severely limited my belief in myself."

Nicole of California recalls a priest in her church who was having an affair with a woman in the community. "She was banished from the city in shame. He was transferred. Again, I questioned the hold of his power as a man over a woman while still practicing his vow of celibacy. . . . His weekly sermons in church were about hell and sins, and he especially denounced woman as the cause of the fall of man in the Garden of Eden. Therefore, it was indirectly embedded into my female thinking that I, as a young woman, was at fault for all of man's problems on earth. . . . It was a typical guilt trip on the female to explain away man's temporary loss of power.

"Today, this guilt enters my marriage at times. I am conditioned to think I am less than man, therefore I must struggle harder than he to be a respectable person. . . . I must work twice as hard—even harder—than a man doing the same work. . . . I feel these . . . misrepresentations of a priest/man have left me scarred with anger and frustration despite my many successful and superb achievements in this lifetime." She summarizes: "The Catholic system, from my perspective, has always been catering to the power of man in religion; whereas, the woman was forced to remain in the background as a servant to man and to God. My developmental years . . . experienced the anguish of this biased attitude toward women."

Sara, the IRS clerk in Texas, looks back on "The gospel read on the Feast of the Holy Family [which] tells how a woman should be subservient to her husband. It points out how she has no rights or freedom of choice. The church seems to think this is good and right. It seems to think that women should be mindless, breeding machines.

"While I was growing up in the church, women were not even allowed on the altar, let alone touch the host. I guess we weren't worthy.

"How can the church be so two-faced as to preach love and equality on one hand and have this attitude toward women on the other hand?"

Ginny: "I still can't believe the myths I was taught concerning sexuality—how the woman is always responsible for any sexual act a man might commit, no woman ever gets raped unless she wants to be." This was particularly painful for Ginny because she was molested by her brother for years. "Of course, I was to be a virgin and since I wasn't [due to the incest], no decent man would want to marry me. I was a used, broken vessel. . . . My sister and brother-in-law were luckier. Being very good Catholics, they 'brought thirteen children into the world.' . . . Even to this day, she is the most respected member of the family" for that accomplishment, one highly valued by the church.

Lily's comments include her belief that, "This institution is a relentless machine of control of minds and bodies. It hates and fears women because *we* create the race, thereby giving the lie to their foremost fantasy of a male creator-god in the sky balancing out the male death-god (Jesus Christ) on earth. The Catholic church is the enemy, implacable enemy, of women past, present, and to come." She adds, "Women must tell the truth about their lives. This truth will shatter the institutions . . . which are founded on the dehumanizing of women, and financed with the stolen labor of women." Lily sees the church *versus* women as an epic struggle, and perhaps she is right.

Connie avows, "The attitude of the church toward women is insufferable. Have children, even if you can't support them; that really irritates me. I wish priests could marry, then they might understand a few of our problems. 'Stay home, devote your life to your family'—bah, humbug!"

Society, of course, provided a major backdrop to what went on in the church in your childhood. It is as if the Catholic hierarchy has placed another layer of sexism on top of what our culture already provides.

Mary: Ally or Enemy?

The Blessed Mother, the Virgin Mary, Mary the Holy Mother—all of these names are used to identify the person called Christ's human mother. She is held in highest esteem by some of the surveyed women, denigrated by others. But the church positions Mary as the model for girls and women to follow, as described by Kelly at the beginning of this chapter. Not sure she wants to be thought of as perfect like Mary, Cyndy observes that, "A pedestal is no different than a ball and chain if you can't move."

Patricia says, "What a confusing role model the Virgin Mary was to me as a girl! Suffering was a 'gift' from God in her life, supposedly, so therefore I should want or like to suffer? My church told me that a woman should be passive, a virgin, and self-sacrificing. At the same time, in the early '70s, from my newly graduated teachers and on the TV and radio, I heard that women should be revolutionary, should burn their bras, should speak out, should liberate themselves from men's oppression! And then on Sundays, I'd be back in church, hearing how wives should serve their husbands and children, how they should be meek and submissive. Helen Reddy sang . . . 'I am woman, hear me roar!' but the church choir sang of 'Silent Night . . . Virgin, tender and mild.' "

"All the women we were told to look up to seemed like wimps to me," adds another woman. "I was attracted to Mary Magdelene, the only woman in the bunch who had any balls, it seemed to me. Mary the Virgin Mother seemed so flaccid: impregnated in fear, giving birth to a son she knew from the start she would lose, never complaining. She was the shining example held up to us, the Queen of the May, the Mother of us all."

The image of Mary, so powerfully enforced by the church at every turn, was the model for girls, as recalled by another of the women: "meek, mild, polite, Christian."

Katrina asks, "If we are created in God's image, and we are male and female, mustn't God have both characteristics, too? Why has the church denied that, and relegated the female to a lowly place, not part of the main group—their Trinity—but 'just' as mother, necessary but subservient to the Almighty Male? Four is wholeness—include her in with the other three!" Traditional Catholics would find this concept shocking: those Catholics who count themselves among the "cult for Mary" are already outcasts.

Denying Their Own Spirituality: "Catholic Woman Syndrome"

Anita, the nanny in Massachusetts, "had a deep spirituality grounded in nature but that never seemed good enough. I wanted desperately to buy into the religion, to prove myself, to get approval from others to bolster my poor self-esteem. . . . I struggled to accept the tenets of male supremacy that permeated the church and society. . . . I read the biographies of saints, especially women, who gave their lives for their God. I spent my recess in grade school either volunteering to guard the votive candles in the church from vandals, or washing dishes in the teachers' convent. I was disgustingly pious to prove my faith, really masking the logical doubts and anxieties from everyone, trying to live up to a falsehood . . . and my struggles were a part of growing holier. If only I could hang onto my beliefs, I would be stronger for the suffering."

What Anita describes here, as she is telling us of her spirituality, is what I call the "Catholic Woman Syndrome," when a woman simply cannot do enough, so she must do it all, and underneath it all, she is doing it all out of fear. The fear is that she will not gain approval. These are women who do not take sick days, even when very ill; who apologize and accept blame, even when they are not at fault. Social workers and therapists should include in their initial interview with a woman client some questions about religious upbringing; being raised Catholic would add some insight to their work with the client whom many would call "co-dependent."

One other woman notes, "If, as that nun told me [long ago], women are the spiritual leaders of the family, then let us have a voice!"

Phyllis, the restaurant owner and mother in Ohio, asks, "What makes those prophets' religious experiences any better or more valid than my own? And yet I was taught to ignore my own."

Another woman who replied is angry "at being denied the chance to participate liturgically. At being made to feel that my sexuality was something to be overcome rather than something in which to exult. At being given the overwhelming example that only women who denied their sexuality completely were given any modicum of power within the church."

Ginny recalls her religious training, and the position of religious women within the church itself. "Our spirituality was very masculine. We were to be soldiers of Christ, battling against the wiles of the flesh, the world, and Satan. We were given more male saints to emulate than women: Sts. Benedict, Ignatius, Joseph, Francis, Bernard."

Holly declares, "I don't believe that women can *be* Catholic. Our level is 'semi-Catholic.' While men are 'sons,' we are 'hand-maidens.' While men can communicate with God, we 'need' them to bridge the gap between our femaleness and God. Although my brothers and father were not required to follow any of the church's precepts, I was required to follow *all* of them."

Jennifer "wanted to be an altar [person] so badly. Most of the boys in my class weren't all that interested in doing that religious stuff, and had to be coerced by the nuns [to serve on the altar]. I envied them, but there was no way possible for me to share in the mass that way."

Jimi ponders women being totally involved in Catholic church liturgy. "In later years when I heard about churches with mixed and female choirs I thought about what a difference it could make to girls and women to be included. . . . I always thought women should be able to be priests and bishops . . . even pope."

"My debts to God are a private matter, and I do not have to have a man/priest intercede for me," Nicole asserts. "Also, the church has not been supportive of women's modern needs and requests; for example, abortion, women serving as priests, or modern-day birth control methods. The power of Man, not God, still exists! God is merely used as a backdrop to any of man's rulings. And this infuriates me! When one sees the ceremonies of the pope, where are the nuns (women)? . . . Are they not . . . responsible for . . . sustaining the life of the Catholic traditions? After all, have they not also trained both boys and girls to become Catholics, mostly in classrooms—longer hours than a priest would dare address? I see no rewards for the female!"

Geraldine of Washington, D.C., believes, "A Catholic girlhood is as crippling as the foot binding of Chinese girls. . . . Perhaps worst is the constant concept of the ideal female as intercessor, the one who asks her *son*, she who 'prays for us sinners now and at the hour of our death.' "

Annmarie, the student in New York, has a pessimistic view. "Nothing would change in their liturgy if women [suddenly] weren't in the church," she says. She visited home one holiday and noticed "it would not have made a difference if women were present or not. Nothing pertained to the women." The exclusive language of the liturgy frustrated her "almost to the point of tears."

She adds, "The patriarchal tradition devalued the women" early in the church, for example, portraying Mary Magdelene as a prostitute. And "women serve in the traditional roles of playing the organ, fixing the altar with flowers, babysitting the children in the church basement. Men are the priests, altar boys, lectors, eucharistic ministers, ushers, greeters, and money collectors."

Jennifer says, "For years I felt liturgically neutered. I was unable to take an active role in the mass and always felt like an isolated participant. I left the church in my mid-twenties, so as a mature adult I have never been part of a Catholic congregation. I have friends who are still active, however, and I see them being angry at the role of women in the church."

Joan is a thirty-five-year-old divorced mother of two and a computer operator in Ohio. She agrees with Jennifer. "I have always been disappointed that women weren't allowed to become priests. The strongest individuals I knew were invariably women, often nuns, some of whom would have been dynamic priests, admirable priests fully capable of carrying on the work of Christ. It has been a terrible injustice, not only to those women who aspire to the priesthood, but to the people who have missed out on the excellent pastoral leadership of those women."

And Ricki of Illinois cites this restriction: "The part that bothered me most was that I was interested as a child in developing my spirituality in everyday life, while this did not seem to be of any interest to my brother [who was an altar boy]."

Reverend Laurel Sheridan, minister of All Souls Unitarian Universalist Church in Braintree, Massachusetts, tells a wonderful story about a wedding ceremony she officiated along with a Catholic priest; the couple wanted both of them there.

The priest, more openminded and risk-taking than many of his peers, had no problem performing the ceremony in a Catholic church with Rev. Sheridan at the altar with him. In order to put on her robes, Laurel was shown to a room near the sanctuary by a nun, who offered to help her change.

As Rev. Sheridan slipped her white robe over her head, let it drop, and smoothed it out, the nun's eyes grew large. Then the minister placed her red stole, with a multitude of religious symbols, around her neck. She looked at the woman facing her. The nun was looking admiringly at Laurel's robe and the stole with the symbols, and with a kindly longing in her eyes and voice, said to Laurel, "You look so beautiful."

What was going through the nun's mind—and what was she feeling with her heart—at that moment?

A footnote to the story is that when Rev. Sheridan went to the altar to join the priest, he was wearing the exact white robe and red stole the minister was wearing. How much more alike need they have been?

Polly, the restoration artisan in Massachusetts, observes, "Popes, cardinals, bishops, and priests have no right to deny a woman who feels that she has been called to the priesthood. There is something inherently wrong with a religion that denies women the right to worship God as they see fit." Today Polly is studying to become an Episcopalian priest.

In some cases, the women tried to change the church from within before they gave up and left. MaryAnn "tried organizing child care during church services as far back as the early 1960s and was rebuffed. I also tried to initiate reforms in the catechism classes during the summers and after school for kids attending public schools, and was held down. Priests also seemed to feel threatened by me. When I taught briefly in a Catholic grade school, I had a long discussion with the parish priest about how the individual's relationship with Christ should not be gainsayed by the priest, and was totally rejected. It was at this point that I broke completely with the church."

Women Should Suffer

Beth had an abusive husband, whom she eventually left. "The priest told me 'you cannot dissolve your marriage; you must put up with your husband.' I could only conclude that the burden of goodness is on the woman." Today she is divorced with five grown children, and is a businesswoman in Massachusetts.

Others agree with her: Abby says her first marriage was "bad, bad. . . . I wanted out but [Catholic] women were supposed to be long-suffering and if you love someone long enough and hard enough, everything will be OK. I was mentally and physically abused." To her, as it has been to other Catholic women, the message was that the burden for change was on the woman. "The Catholic church thinks it's never too early to preach and teach shame and guilt!" Barbara of Texas endured a physically abusive husband for seventeen years because, "I thought this was my punishment for being so sinful. Guilt, guilt, guilt."

Cassie is a forty-nine-year-old store clerk in Louisiana, divorced with three children. Cassie's husband took literally his role in the family according to the church. "It was a horrible, horrible marriage," she says. "I played by the rules—he didn't. Once I came home from mass to find him angry that I had slipped out and not awakened him before I left so he could have sex. . . . So he slapped me around and raped me. At the time I was about three months pregnant."

" 'Pray, pay, and obey' was the dictum governing the lives of Irish women— nuns and mothers alike," declares Tina. ". . . We prayed, we gave our weekly [donation] envelopes, and no one was aware that the stories of hell and God's wrath were creating in us the terrified angry victims of criticism who would find it very difficult to assume the liberated woman role expected in the 1980s."

Judy of Colorado says, "My husband had a mental illness and I stayed married to him for twenty-three years. Every two years we went through five to six months of a psychotic episode. The church's teaching of 'marriage is forever' kept me there that long. I was a wonderful Christian Catholic martyr. I let the church walk all over me, my husband walk all over me, and my children walk all over me, as well. Their [the church's] interpretation of 'acceptance' is now sickening to me. There were times when I felt second to everyone." This feeling is one major piece of Catholic shrapnel.

Terry notes, "There seems to be an unspoken message coming through to me that Catholic women are expected to suffer, in silence even."

Nuns: Fear and Sympathy

There is no shortage of nun horror stories in Catholic folklore. As mentioned earlier, these incidents do not generate chuckles from the women surveyed here. Some of the samples are chilling. They show how a system that deprives people of their power can drive those same people to unacceptable behaviors.

"When I get together with other people who were raised Catholic," Janet says, "a usual topic of conversation is how mean the nuns were. They hit us with knitting needles . . . , and used overshoes to hit boys about the ears." MaryAnn's fourth-grade teacher "had us eat paste just to see 'if we were dumb enough to do it.' "

Bernice could not remember her Latin vocabulary, and was getting Cs instead of As on her tests, which infuriated the nun. "Her method to help me remember the Latin words? She stood me up at the blackboard and banged my head into it. The next day, I did get that A and the nun proudly proclaimed that her method worked."

When Evelyn, the married homemaker in South Dakota, was in the second grade, her nun interpreted Evelyn's slowness as obstinacy. "Sister placed my fingers spread-eagled across my desk. Then she beat them with a ruler to her satisfaction."

During World War II, Holly "was enrolled [in Catholic school] and placed in the first grade even though I was just five. Each day I was 'punished' (tape on my mouth, made to kneel on dried peas) because I had a German last name and had to pay for the people who were suffering in Europe. One day, I was sitting on the curb watching the other children play in the street. The nun (my teacher) came to me and ordered me into the street. I apologized and told her that my mother forbade me to play in the street. . . . She picked me up by the collar and pants and threw me headfirst into the street." She says she went to public school instead after this occurred, "and attended release time classes. . . . The nuns *repeatedly* told us that we were going to hell because we went to public school."

Barbara remembers how "the nuns made me kneel on soda caps nailed [upside down] on a board" for punishment. Her mother did not want to question the nuns. But "years later, my grandmother was horrified to learn of this. 'Why didn't you say something?' my grandmother asked. I said, 'I didn't know the difference. I was just a kid.' " Being "just a kid," and suffering such abuse, fuels the anger of many of these women.

This corporal punishment was doled out by the priests, whose example the nuns followed. "A favorite punishment for boys who were unruly in class," according to Bernice, "was to put them in the closet or under the desk. At the nearby boys' Catholic school, one boy was put into the coat closet. It was never clear whether the brother [priest] stuck the boy in there by his tie. But the boy died by strangulation. It was declared an accidental death and the brother was sent to another school to teach."

The torment was not only physical. The nuns Jill of New Jersey had would not let her use her own name. "I was told it was not a real name [of a saint]. I was forced to be called Joan and reprimanded when I wrote 'Jill.' . . . I received more slaps and beatings at school than at home. I never told my mother and father about it because as the nuns were administering the punishment, they warned me that my parents would consider me bad if I told, and they wouldn't love me."

Tina can still see and hear the nuns saying to her class, "Now girls! The College Board scores are in. We used to think you were all just bad. Now, we know you are *bad* and *stupid*."

Hillary is a designer and married mother of two, who is in her thirties and lives in Connecticut. She remembers, "At fifteen years old I gave birth to a child, and gave it up for adoption through Catholic Charities. I had no counseling, no preparation for the emotional trauma of the whole ordeal. So, while I'm in the hospital, a priest shows up—to take my confession! I was horrified at the thought of the ordeal being reduced to how many times I had sex—and to say a few prayers and I would be forgiven. I wept and wailed; I felt so trapped and angry. The nuns and priest thought I was crying out of shame." This sounds like a scene from a psychological horror film.

"The hatred I feel for those nuns who embarrassed and humiliated me will be with me till the day I die," said Kelly. "Those twisted, psychological misfits who were using us to feel powerful have nothing but my enduring hatred." Kelly touches on an important point: power. Because today women understand that the nuns had no real power, except over children, they feel understanding and sympathy for their nuns, despite the terrible stories.

"The nuns were as much prisoners of the times as we were," says Bernice. "They taught us what *they* had been taught was correct. I regret that the nuns were not able to prepare us adequately for the real world."

Susan believes the nuns' behavior "was a control thing. Therefore they were quite vicious to powerless children." She recalls the use of " 'the clicker.' The nuns used this clicking thing to cue all the children's movements [in church]. This made the nun look good, look in control." Susan quotes Gail Sheehy on survival: "Sheehy says that the Cambodians had a smiling, placid exterior which hid emotions of savage fury. I see a parallel with the nuns. . . . As nuns, they had to continue their ongoing repression, denying their feelings."

Ronnie feels "they didn't really know how to relate to people, didn't treat students with as much respect . . . as they should have. Now I feel kind of sorry for them" for their secondary role in the church.

Debbie says "some of them were entirely too strict and took their frustrations out on the kids," but "many of them were dedicated teachers, good, holy women and I must admit that some of my strongest ideals about what a woman should be were formed by those early instructors of mine."

While they can tell horror stories, the women even then were aware of underlying issues. On some level, they were aware of the nuns being caught in a larger system. Also, they were watching the nuns' behavior as women, as behavior to be emulated or rejected.

As part of this awareness, the women, as girls, were keenly

sensitive to the church's messages about the inferiority of nuns especially when compared to male priests.

About priests and nuns, Bernice learned, "Nuns could run the regular religious instruction classes, but a priest was required to come in once a week to make sure those nuns had taught us correctly. Father Jim said, 'The dear sisters are very good, but when it comes to doctrine, God has entrusted this to the priests. Only men can become priests.' How good are priests? According to Father Jim, 'A priest is so respected in heaven, that even the angels bow to him.' " What a powerful image for a child.

Kaye puts it this way: "The nuns, by modelling, always emphasized the superior role of priests." At the time, the nuns' roles were not questioned, even by the nuns.

Jennifer comments on women's versus men's status in the church. "Well, let's begin with the concept of God. Always pictured as a man. And God's son. Priests, all men. It was quite clear that the priests, monsignors, bishops, archbishops, cardinals, and popes had the clout, and they were all men.

"Within each classroom, the nun had the power. However, her power faded into nothing whenever a priest entered the room. It was clear to me that the men had the upper hand."

Jennifer also observed how differently priests and nuns lived. "The inequity of what had to be sacrificed in order to be powerful hit me very hard. Priests were supposed to be celibate. . . . But they lived in the rectory—only two or three of them—they had cars, drank, smoked, told dirty jokes on occasion, took vacations. . . . In exchange for celibate life, they received all the power.

"Nuns, on the other hand, gave up their sexuality completely. Their hair . . . and their bodies were encased in head-to-toe black habits that concealed breasts, waists, etc. They were neutered. . . . They lived like carefully supervised bees in a hive of a convent."

MaryAnn of Missouri describes all this: "It seemed the priests 'submitted' to the church and got promotions and power; the women 'submitted' and got used. . . . I wanted to be a priest . . . and knew I never could."

Maggie says, "Occasionally for daily mass there were no boys available for servers and I remember the nuns giving the Latin responses from the lay side of the communion rail [instead of from the altar side]. Knowing some of the boys as well as I did, I knew they were not particularly holy or even nice. I often wondered why Christ's 'bride' could only be close to the altar to clean or arrange flowers while the bratty boys could be up there right by the priest."

What about from a nun's point of view? Ginny tells us, "[We buy] our own food in the convent but food in the rectory was always provided by the parish budget. We nuns have to take the bus. I resent using public transportation while the priests drive Cadillacs.

"As principal I was totally responsible for the administration of the school, but the pastor's name always appeared on report cards, documents, etc. Only if something went wrong or there was a problem would my name surface. It meant being principal, being full-time eighth-grade teacher, my own secretary, supervisor, so forth, all at the same time with no extra consideration or pay.

"Until my present position, I never had medical insurance or retirement. Sisters were never to get sick (God forbid) and since they would work until they died, they didn't need retirement.

"The inequality continues. . . . The lay woman on staff who has exactly the same job description as I do . . . gets $25,279 a year. I get $9,900 a year.

"So if you think women in the church have it bad, remember,

there is one group lower: nonpersons often referred to as the 'good sisters.' "

Chris notes the "clear message from the start is that Catholicism is made for men; women are there to produce more Catholics." She adds, "Men's opinions are the ones the church hears. I think it would be wonderful to belong to a church that listened to men *and* women, and someday I'll find that church. But until then the male hierarchy who runs the church can have it for themselves."

Episcopalian Priests

Q. 451: What is Holy Orders?

Answer: Holy Orders is the sacrament through which men receive the power and grace to perform the sacred duties of bishops, priests, and other ministers of the Church.

Q. 452: What are some of the requirements that a man may receive Holy Orders worthily?

Answer: That a man may receive Holy Orders worthily it is necessary: first, that he be in the state of grace and be of excellent character; second, that he have the prescribed age and learning; third, that he have the intention of devoting his life to the sacred ministry; fourth, that he be called to Holy Orders by his bishop.
—*The New Baltimore Catechism* (p. 193)

When asked about the 1993 Vatican decision to admit into the Roman Catholic priesthood several married Episcopalian priests who were opposed to women serving as priests in the Anglican church, the women were outraged.

"Here we go again," says Kathleen, the mother of one and

a high school teacher in Ohio. "We'll relax the rules for the men, but never relax them for the women! . . . The celibate priesthood is an unattractive career to many men, so to boost the thinning ranks of Catholic priests, the church has decided to 'import' them. What next: Lutheran priests? Methodist priests?" She continues, "Why not consider the logical next step—allow women to be ordained."

Maggie asks, "They will do anything to get more priests, won't they? . . . It prolongs [the time before] the dreadful day that they have to take Catholic women into the priesthood. I think they'd rather the world ended! As *they* know it, it *would*. The church is saying: 'We'll accept you—as long as you are opposed to what we're opposed to! No thinking for yourself.' "

"Is the Vatican scared women will take over their dictatorship?" wonders Donna, a thirty-year-old married registered nurse in Minnesota with one child. Hillary of Connecticut provides an answer: "They just can't handle it if their power or control . . . is threatened in any way."

Abby believes that the church "is running out of people who are willing to buy into . . . the priest's lifestyle, so a few married priests won't hurt anything, just as long as women don't think that they can come in. The Vatican will put up with a few married priests, and they can put up with a priest as a sexual person, as long as they [all] can still be misogynists, and not have a problem with how the church does not treat men and women equally. It goes along with the Roman Catholic misogynist view." One cannot help but think of the phrase "united in their misogyny" as the Vatican tried to forge stronger links with anti-feminist Islamic leaders in a stance against population control, as was seen in September 1994 during the United Nations conference on population.

Chris calls this new recruiting attempt by the church, which claims thirty-five Anglican priests to have already "switched" (*Boston Globe,* December 7, 1993), "Pathetic. . . . This is a last-ditch effort being made only because the priesthood is dwindling. I think the Episcopalian priests would be treated as second-class citizens. This . . . reflects what must be fear of the church losing power. It is also an insult to Catholic women everywhere, because it reminds them that they still aren't worthy of leadership in the church. Increase the population for us, and don't ask any questions . . . yes, that's still the role women play in the church."

4

Sex, Birth Control, and Abortion

Q. 274: Are mere thoughts about impure things always sinful in themselves?

Answer: Mere thoughts about impure things are not always sinful in themselves, but such thoughts are dangerous.

Q. 275: When do thoughts about impure things become sinful?

Answer: Thoughts about impure things become sinful when a person thinks of an unchaste act and deliberately takes pleasure in so thinking, or when unchaste desire or passion is aroused and consent is given to it.
—*The New Baltimore Catechism* (p. 119)

I knew there would be a strong reaction to the survey question: "Describe how you may not agree with the church on birth control, abortion, and related issues." The women's comments here reveal the depth of their resentment toward the church's meddling in so personal an area of their lives; their remarks are also laced with resentment that they "bought the church's line" for so long.

The Church's Obsession with Sex

Why has the church been so concerned with the sex lives of its members? Certainly theologians would point to various personages in Catholic history. But what about today?

Susan remembers, "Sister Marie David told us not to use toilet paper because to touch ourselves was impure. We were little kids, we didn't know what the hell she was talking about! So I 'drip dried' for years. . . . We were also told 'no hands under your blankets,' but we never knew why. It's a bizarre sickness, this 'your body is filthy' mentality."

Jennifer thinks back to "The first overt mention of sex [which] was in the eighth grade. Our teacher was the principal of the grade school. . . . Two years earlier, I had seen her slap my sixth-grade teacher in front of the class because she dared to question something the principal said. She used to take delight in weaving horrible stories for us about Communists. They were coming, she insisted. They would nail priests and nuns to the doorways and blood would run in the streets. Nice stuff, huh?

"She also insisted that 50 percent of the class would surely go to hell. I always knew I was in the damned group.

"This same nun would have the boys leave the room and then talk to us about sex without ever mentioning the word and giving no explicit details. Her main goal was to instill in us a mighty fear and dread and to ensure that sex looked very unattractive. She depicted boys as wild animals, unable to control their passions. Girls, she said, were more able to control their urges and were responsible for safeguarding their purity. Nothing about birth control. Only about consequences."

Tina of New York recalls "the principal's reaction to the illegitimate child of a high school classmate: the nun said, 'The little girl looks perfectly normal. No one would ever know.' "

She adds that she was also told by the nuns, " 'Those girls who are sexy—they are the ones the boys will "use," but never marry. You, when you are eighteen, will be the one they will marry. You are not sexy, but why would you want to be?' I am thirty-eight and still waiting."

Nan wonders, "What business does the church have in sex education, marriages, birth control, living together before marriage? How can a priest know all this if he's celibate?" Today Nan, 45, is a married mother of four and a shop owner in Minnesota.

Maggie recollects a Catholic magazine article that reinforced the concept of no premarital sex. "An article in the *St. Anthony's Messenger* newsletter said if a man had sex with a prostitute, he became 'one' with her—apparently this only happens with the first sex act a person experiences—and explained how horrified the man will be in heaven to find out he is one flesh with a whore. Horrors! I went through much guilt thinking about the one boy I had sex with before my husband."

Jill was taught: "All kids were expected to abstain from sex. . . . But those girls who were sexually active were ridiculed and marked if the nuns found out about it." She also recalls that she learned that one particular phase of life—puberty—was the most dangerous. "Anything to do with sex was viewed as sinful and people who as much as held hands or kissed were considered sinful. When we were ninth graders, we had a priest come in once a week who lectured about the evils of our budding sexuality. If we had sexual feelings we were already condemning ourselves."

Bernice learned there was "an allowed activity: holding hands. We were taught: 'You know you are right for each other if he respects you enough to do no more than hold your hand. The couples who go to Communion together every Sunday are those who are sanctified by God.' " Her teenage years were those of "sanctified courtship." The responsibility of purity rested with the girl: "We were not allowed to date until we were sixteen. But before we reached that age we had a class called 'Catholic Family Living,' in which we learned the dos and don'ts of Catholic dating. It was common for girls to wear panty girdles in those days. Sister Mary Bartholomew said, 'Remember girls, always wear a panty girdle on a date and keep your knees together.' "

Paula, a waitress in Massachusetts and mother of two, maintains: "These issues . . . are personal ones and a church thinking they have that much power over you is a frightening thing."

Glenna says, "The Catholic church's obsession with the sex lives of its members I find both fascinating and infuriating." No doubt Glenna means this is fascinating because despite the volumes that the church speaks about sex and reproduction, sex is something the hierarchy denies itself. (Could it be they *are* so obsessed because they do not allow it for themselves?!) And infuriating because despite the hierarchy's lack of knowledge about things sexual they position themselves as experts on such real-life situations.

It is known among those growing up with Catholic friends or relatives that they could count on the Catholic kids, especially those in Catholic school, to know the best dirty jokes. Could the emphasis on suppressing sexuality have had the opposite effect that the church desired?

An answer comes from Sara of Texas, who says a more moderate way of teaching young people about sex would have been more effective. "Staying a virgin was drummed into me as much as guilt was. Guilt was used constantly, teaching me this [remain a virgin] as well as the 'fear of Hell.' I don't know what attitudes the boys were taught. All I know is that I never understood why everyone made such a big deal of this issue. Their intimidation didn't work very well because I wasn't a virgin when I got married. Maybe if logic instead of guilt had been used as a teaching tool I may have listened better."

Cathy says she will teach her two children about birth control in this way: " 'You can choose when to have a baby. A baby is a gift. You do not have the right to impose a life on your child that is not loving and nurturing. Can you do that at sixteen?' What a difference [teaching that] than saying 'to stop procreation is a sin.' Or no matter how screwed up you are, you must bring every child into this world.

". . . It (sex) may feel good and there is a purpose—understand it—enjoy it and be responsible."

Blame the Girl

In the last few years American society largely has turned away from the notion that the victim is the guilty party in a questionable situation. But the church has its own rules.

Ginny remembers: "Boys were so lucky. Since girls were always to be in control, if a boy had an 'impure' thought or feeling he could always blame the girl. It was *always* her fault. This is only one of the myths I was taught." And the priest who abused her only reinforced this belief by commanding that *she* go to confession. Ginny adds: "Sex—an unmentionable word. I still am angry that I was fifty-five years old before I was able to say, 'I was sexually abused. I am not a bad person.' Although I was only five when my eighteen-year-old brother began to abuse me, I was blamed and told I was a bad girl. It is *always* the girl's fault. There is no such thing as rape. A girl gets what she asks for."

Cyndy of Pennsylvania tells about an experience in the confessional. "I had been petting heavily with my boyfriend. I hadn't actually gone all the way with him, but we had gotten close. Feeling guilty, I confessed my sin of heavy petting. *And the priest called me a slut! A slut! Me*—who had stopped my boyfriend, much to the consternation of both of us. *Me*, who was still a virgin, unlike all of my friends, *me*, a slut. *Ha!* I could see that all my efforts were wasted.

"He didn't say anything about the boy—not a single bad name. It was, of course, my fault. Boys couldn't be expected to control themselves—after all, they had natural urges. (Then what were all those urges *I* had?)"

MaryAnn recalls the same treatment. "This inequity did not even occur to me until later years. I suffered under the guilt of my desires for so long that I did not emerge from this fog until the 1980s."

Chris attempts to figure out the church's thinking: "I feel that the church wants women to be inferior because the men who run it are insecure. I don't think women feel the need to prove themselves sexually like men do, because they know who they are, much more so than men. Since men run the church, they feel much more sympathetic toward the fragile egos of other men and therefore they excuse sexual activity in men, whereas women's desires are unsympathetically ignored. All of these underlying feelings are covered up by the church's claim to want women to be like the Virgin Mary. It is fine to proclaim things in the name of God, but it is hypocritical to use God as an excuse to boost egos, which is just what the church does."

Abby remembers what she calls "absolution in advance" for boys: "My boyfriend said that the priest told him that priests could forgive boys at the Saturday afternoon confessions for what the boys were going to do on Saturday night, but they could not do the same for girls."

At times this "blame the victim" mentality had its impact

on the women's self-esteem, even in nonsexual situations. Loretta says she "grew up very ashamed of who I was. I felt unworthy. I felt dirty and unattractive because I had a female body which might be an 'occasion of sin' to a boy. . . . Sex was always dirty, except under special conditions (i.e., when a married man and woman had sex and a pregnancy resulted). Sex was not to be enjoyed by women; 'good' women didn't have sexual feelings. And, women were responsible to draw the line because men just couldn't help themselves. They had desires and urges so strong they were absolved of all responsibility."

Kathleen of Ohio talks about a particular pre-cana experience. "In 1972 my fiancé and I went to our premarriage interview with the priest. When it was over (we were interviewed together and separately), my fiancé remarked that there were some rather strange questions asked. Since I thought the questions were rather mundane (Are you aware of the church's teaching on birth control? Will the children be raised Catholic? etc.), I asked him what he meant. He said the priest had asked him if *I* had ever engaged in group sex or promiscuous sex. I was flabbergasted! He never asked *me* that about my husband-to-be! Why was there a double standard? Church law states premarital sex is a sin for anyone, not just women!!!"

Susan of Michigan recalls that "the priests told boys, 'Don't do it, but if you do. . . .' Girls were told, 'Don't.' " She also remembers a nun "whispering to us [girls in class] about 'the sacred marriage act.' We never knew what she meant, but she always whispered it." It is Susan's view that "virginity is a highly overrated commodity." One more adds, "Our nuns told us that if you even French kissed, you would go to hell."

Catholic Roulette

Darla, the travel agent from California, recalls "one young mother of four young ones who bitterly said she could wallpaper her house with all the [rhythm birth control] charts she kept and here are four children to prove it doesn't work.

"I can never forgive the church for such an unnecessary burden placed on us. We had two children, born in 1957 and 1959, then played Catholic Roulette (the rhythm method) until I had our third child in 1969. I nearly had a nervous breakdown. What if I had another one in nine months? in two years? How can I handle all these children? Will my teeth fall out, I wondered, will I have retarded children when I'm forty? The only comfort the church provided was 'God will provide.' "

Holly says, "When I married, I got pregnant immediately! Our first child was born thirteen months after we were married, and even though I practiced rhythm, I became pregnant again. I lost the baby after two months. The doctors gave me birth control pills to help regulate my period. I was not allowed absolution [when I confessed this]. I lost four babies and finally carried one to full term. After she was born, I went to confession and again was denied absolution because I had only two children. The fact that I had lost four, and nearly died from this cycle of miscarriages, was not valid to the priest. That was the last time I ever went to confession."

Adrianne of Texas describes herself as "not a virgin; I am monogamous and use birth control. I have no qualms about ignoring these religious rules, which were invented by male chauvinists like John Paul and the various popes." She goes on to say: "It is wrong that the church can tell me, 'If you want to have sex, get married and use the rhythm method.' Too bad for me if I get pregnant and have to quit school; after all, it is the man's job to earn a living, right? Not only are these views blatantly sexist, they are economically unrealistic. Even with my father earning a good living of $43,000 a year, my mother needs to work in order to afford the tuition bills for my two younger brothers. Certainly my mother cannot afford to put her reproductive potential into the hands of fate, and most women are in even less favorable economic circumstances. As a biologist, I know how well the rhythm method works; in fact, both my sister and I are living proof of its inadequacy as a method of controlling birth."

"Women Should Not Enjoy Sex"

Bernice was taught that "Women should not enjoy sex. The act of sex is a gift of a woman to her husband. During the sex act, a woman should keep herself chaste by thinking about other things. For example, planning a special dinner for her family."

Judy of Colorado learned, "Sex was certainly not for my enjoyment. Sex was for procreation only. The man had to enjoy it by the nature of it all. Sex was not for women to enjoy. If she did enjoy it there was something not quite right. The church also taught that the woman could not say no to her husband no matter when he asked. If she said no and he masturbated, it was her fault. Somehow it was never okay for a woman to ask for sex."

Lily of Missouri maintains, "The bottom line [of the church's philosophy is]: 'Women exist at the pleasure of and for the service of men (males), because their [men's] bodies (penises) are imitative of the diety's.' Self-hatred is inculcated and fostered in little girls and women. . . . And the endless sermons, talks, and texts on female impurity and provocation; and no talks on male abuse and violence toward women and children." One wonders if today those priests, looking back, are at all embarrassed by this unbalanced stance.

Sara reiterates what some of the women have already said here: "I was taught for as long as I can remember that the only good reason to have sex was for reproduction and thus bringing members into the church. I was never taught by anyone that sex was an extension of love between two people. I was never taught it was enjoyable. All I knew was that married people did it and they were supposed to have as many babies as possible."

Connie, the sixty-three-year-old nurse in Florida, agrees: "It was always understood that sex was for procreation, until I married and found out differently." And Paula, the waitress and married mother of two in Massachusetts, scoffs, "Sex as a duty and not a biological impulse is absurd. Sex is joy and pleasure . . . sex is natural and should be understood as that, . . . it is part of life."

Margo notes, "Sex was not for my own joy and pleasure. I didn't even learn how to masturbate until I was thirty. It was fabulous! God, what I had been missing!"

Totally outside the realm of church-prescribed heterosexuality are the two lesbian women who answered the survey. One, Jimi, says, "Because I am a lesbian and comfortable with that identity, I disagree with the church in its stand on homosexuality."

Hurting the Marriage

Repeated pregnancies took their toll on marriages, according to the women.

Glenna asserts: "I have seen too many women's minds and bodies taxed beyond their limits by countless pregnancies and the next-to-impossible task of raising far too many children while attempting to see to the needs of their husbands at the same time. In many cases, the husband's life was ruined as well."

On the subject of strained marriages, Glenna believes that many times there was a clash between the man's conscience and the woman's knowledge of the physical burden of yet another baby. "In some cases, I saw insensitive husbands who were all too ready to leave the burden of child raising to a distraught wife. While one of my friends, after her fifth pregnancy and many related health problems, was trying to make the decision to have a tubal ligation, against the church's wishes, of course, her husband commented that he was sorry if she had to have a baby every year, but he simply could not, in good conscience, support her decision."

Darla believes: "The biggest and worst thing they have chained people with" is the ban on birth control, and it is "unforgivable. How many young (and old) couples tried to deny their sexual nature as a 'sacrifice' but really it was to avoid an unwanted pregnancy?"

Kaye remembers older women in her family. "From as early as I can remember, Catholic aunts were miserable over fears of pregnancy, being pregnant, miscarrying, aborting, fighting against sex with their husbands. . . . I certainly had a grim view of what it is to be a woman (all pain, blood, gore) and be pregnant. I've never had children; although I thought I wanted them, I had a dread of pregnancy."

Some relate how mixed messages—here, church versus family—made its mark. Anne was taught that, "Sex, in the eyes of the church, is only for married people, and even then, it is merely to be tolerated in order to create something worthwhile: a child. This always bothered me—even as a young child because my parents had never told me that it was bad or dirty or subhuman, but the church did. Needless to say, I became confused about the issue."

Judy talks of the effect of the birth control ban on her husband, after they were counseled to try birth control to improve their sexual relations. "We tried using condoms and my husband had a difficult time letting go of the guilt."

"A Baby Mill for the Church"

Some of the women say bitterly that women are important to the church strictly for their ability to have children so that the church has a constant supply of "customers." Anne alleges, "Woman, in the eyes of the church, is a baby-machine and a nurturer, nothing more or less." She elaborates: "I absolutely detest the church's position on the issues of birth control and abortion because what it is saying, in essence, is that a woman is bound, it is her duty to refuse her own will, to ignore her own health and happiness, and to relinquish herself to God and man. She must serve them by using her own body, regardless of her own wishes and needs, to create babies. . . . To this day, the archaic stance the church takes on the subjects of birth control and abortion is appalling and hurtful, as well as detrimental to every Catholic woman's well-being."

Irene of California pointedly says, "I went to an all-girls Catholic high school. Girls weren't encouraged to *be anything* other than good Catholic baby-maker wives. I am so angry because I know I could have had a great contributing career with a little direction and encouragement. Instead I was taught some basic survival skills—typing, bookkeeping, and cake-making, and I'm grateful I at least learned that because now at least I can earn a substandard living as an accounting clerk, because the baby-making-wife career fell through."

Donna concludes: "I don't find anything wrong with using birth control or having sex before marriage. Since the Catholic church is so adamantly against all of this, I can't . . . continue to call myself Catholic. My beliefs are different."

Susan says, "The men [of the church] are outraged that women can [now]control their uteruses. This means a loss of power to them."

Geraldine agrees, and elaborates: "Catholicism thrives and grows among the poor and ignorant, and is overcome by education and economic well-being. Control over reproduction thus does certainly reduce the need of Catholic comfort. . . . So the apparent Catholic struggle for the 'Right to Life' is . . . actually a struggle for the survival of the Catholic religion. . . . In a religion that outlaws birth control and abortion—and divorce—the role of women is obvious. My mother had a baby every fifteen months until she was a physical wreck and died at forty-eight. . . . Her religion even resisted anesthesia during childbirth for almost fifty years."

MaryAnn says: "I knew early on that if priests could have children the doctrine would change quickly."

The church's view of the family is akin to what one used to see on "Ozzie and Harriet," "Donna Reed," and even the more recent "Cosby Show": a father, a mother, and children. In the church's fantasy family, the man is a steady and present provider, the woman does not work outside the home and gladly welcomes each easy (of course) pregnancy after pregnancy, and the children all go to Catholic school and college.

Where widowed or single women fit is never mentioned. One assumes they should be nuns. The concepts of homosexuality and divorce are not part of the church's view, at least as prescribed by the Vatican: divorce should not take place, and homosexuality is tolerated only if the person is celibate.

But these views reflect a church that is out of touch with the reality that the women here talk about, and that you have experienced. Catholic couples, like other couples, find that there are differences between them that only divorce can solve. And homosexuality is not a quirk or personality characteristic that a person could change or suppress, even if they wanted to.

Also in this perfect Catholic world, sex before or outside of marriage does not exist. And if abortion were outlawed, abortions would no longer be performed. The hierarchy ignores the fact that married women, for example, compose one-third of the women who seek legal abortions each year, and that illegal abortions existed for centuries before it was legalized, and will again if legal abortions are ever denied. Indeed, there are caustic bumper stickers that pronounce, "If men could get pregnant, abortion would be a sacrament." (Another version reads, "If priests could get pregnant. . . .") While that may be stretching it a bit, many of these women would knowingly nod and agree with that sentiment.

Some of the women react angrily to the church's stance on birth control because they have seen how they, or someone they loved and who followed the church's ban on birth control, was hurt by that obedience. One is Adele: "When my mom nearly cracked up during her tenth pregnancy (in thirteen years), I knew I was furious at the Catholic church for its terrible ban on birth control. . . . When my father drowned in 1980 (the oldest child being twenty-one, and the youngest only seven), the difficulty of having ten kids was underlined even more clearly."

And many of the women feel anger that they followed the church's teaching only to see that the reality of being a mother was not the sanctified fantasy in which they had been lead to believe. Cassie of Louisiana says, "What makes me most resentful of the church was that because of my obedience in the matter of birth control I bore two more children for a man I despised and it only made it worse for everyone when the inevitable divorce happened."

Says Kelly: "I was still too stupid to use birth control when I was first married. I had four kids in five years. . . . I am angry that for many years I followed the rules of the Catholic church and now its members do what they want regarding birth control [by ignoring the church]. I know many 'good' Catholics who have had a tubal ligation. I almost died, as well as my son, at his birth—this was the second out of five. I was told by my MD not to have any more children. I had three more because I thought it was a 'sin' to use birth control." The old beliefs must have been strong for Kelly to risk her life.

Bobbie is a thirty-year-old postal clerk in New York, married with no children. She asserts, "Birth control rules are ridiculous. I know a woman with ten children because of it. . . . I cannot and will not discuss my sex life with . . . any priest. It is mine and God's business only!"

Chris gets "so angry when the priest talks about women as objects who deserve no control over their bodies. . . . Men don't have to worry if they get a woman pregnant—they don't have to carry an unwanted child for nine months of their lives. So it's very easy for the all-male Catholic hierarchy to sit back and tell women what to do." She thinks the church's teaching on sex for procreation is "selfish": "The church's views on sex are strictly selfish, I think. All they are worried about is future Catholics. They think as long as sex is accompanied by a woman's pregnancy, it's fine [they say]. But then, if two people have sex to please each other without having a child, it's dirty and wrong. . . . I don't understand how people can subject themselves to this dictatorship claiming to be a religion. If you care for someone, sex is a wonderful way of showing your feelings. But to use it as a weapon, as the church does, makes it sound cheap. . . . I wonder how many children have been born just to please the Vatican. As far as I'm concerned, my sex life is my business."

Cathy questions, "Does the church really believe that rampant baby making teaches respect for life? I personally think the church would fare better saying 'bring God's children into a loving home'—life is too precious to not have direction and control and personal choice."

On disagreeing with the church on birth control, several women make representative comments. They disagree with the church on birth control because of concerns about world population, and because it is an unrealistic stance, given the complexity of life today.

They generally disagree with the church on abortion for reasons including Terry's: "How can a church preach good will while expecting a raped and battered thirteen-year-old not to have an abortion?" They think birth control is preferable to abortion, but believe a woman should be able to obtain safe, legal abortions, as Ronnie says: "No one has the right to tell a woman who can't care for a child that she can't abort that fetus. . . . I am pro-life *and* pro-choice. This is not an incompatible stance."

Sara declares, "I don't feel the church has any right to tell me how many children I should have or what I should do with my body. They don't have to go through the pain of childbirth or the financial strain children cause, let alone the emotional strain. Is it really better to have a baby one doesn't want or can't afford, than to abort it? I don't think so. I think it is morally wrong to bring a baby into the world you can't take care of properly, for whatever the reason.

"What about the young girl who's raped? The church says she must have that baby, even if she puts it up for adoption. . . . Who is the church to pronounce such unreasonable dictates? I think the church has way overstepped its bounds by its stand on abortion and birth control."

"I don't agree [with the church] about birth control because I have seen the end result of too many unwanted children in this world," offers Jill, the counselor in New Jersey. How does she feel about abortion? "While I personally am opposed to it, it is a matter of personal choice."

The shock of reality caused some of the women to change their views on following the church ban on birth control or abortion. Cyndy considered herself a devout Catholic while she was a teenager, and enthusiastically participated in several teen retreat groups. She pushed aside any questions of the church, until her sister came to her for help: "My sister got pregnant. She was fifteen. The boy was a total jerk, poor as sin, and as much of a low-life as possible. I had swallowed whole all the church's teachings on abortion; how it was murder, how the baby was more important than the mother and had a right to live regardless of the circumstances, and so forth. But my sister was pregnant. And only fifteen. My sister would have ruined her whole life if she had had that baby. I could not, and would not, believe that a bunch of cells not even as big as a thumb (no matter how many magnified pictures of bloody parts of fetuses they showed in school) was more important than her whole life. . . . So when my sister came to me in tears, I paid for her abortion."

"My niece had an abortion," says Margo of Vermont. "It was the best answer for her. She was young. I love her just the same."

A few of the women express ambivalence about abortion. Cathy maintains, "Abortion should not be used as a form of birth control. . . . I do think there are times for abortion—incest, rape—

and yet there is a tug at my heart strings that that child, too, is a gift. This is an emotional issue for me."

But Tina adds, "I want to ask the Right to Life ladies their views on capital punishment. How about welfare payments to single mothers. . . . Shouldn't the often sheltered, married, suburban middle-class white Catholic be only too happy to have their tax dollars support such children?"

MaryAnn maintains, "These issues [sex, birth control, abortion] are anguished ones for everyone, but what I resent is women being sacrificed to supply a baby mill for the church because they don't trust God to supply members in other ways. As long as the church remains male dominated, its doctrines will remain not only dehumanizing but actually abusive to women."

Refusing to Be a Cow

Why have all these children in the first place?

To those not raised Catholic, this power, and the women's allegiance to a church teaching—especially one that *is* so personal—is no doubt amazing and mystifying. How could these women bear child after child, their stamina largely provided by what they were taught by their church? What kind of beliefs were these?

An explanation is that the women heard sermons, parables, and stories about their role (and that of men) over and over again from the church. Between kindergarten and high school graduation, a girl might attend weekly mass and Sunday school over 650 times, and if she attended Catholic school, add daily mass and instruction. Consider that this indoctrination was often reinforced by their families, and that these lessons were taught throughout the girl's childhood and adolescence when she is in her most formative years.

Such powerful influences meant that the messages of obedience were taken to heart by the girls, and the danger of disobeying was painted all too clearly in many shades of guilt, a topic explored in more detail in another chapter. The rewards for being a good girl, a good mother—i.e., one with many children—were shown in the obvious comments of admiration by priests and nuns. A look at the darker side of the church's idealized role is provided by Glenna: "My role models as I was growing up were women with large families—several with as many as ten children—and many of whom had had some sort of nervous collapse. These unhappy, overworked women were spoken of in hushed and reverent tones, for they were living their lives as good Catholic women should." In other words, miserable but admired.

But women facing day-to-day reality quietly revolted later in their lives. Says Holly: "I refused to be a cow, and willingly embraced birth control. This opened the door to many other questions. As women tried to do more in the church I became angrier and angrier, and guiltier and guiltier."

Margo asks, "The church isn't paying the bills so how can they tell you the number of kids to have?" She adds: "The church doesn't have the right to tell us about our sex lives with our mate. I wish, I wish I'd had some premarital experiences. . . . I got married at twenty-one. It was a relief [to be able to have sex]. My parents had never told me about sex. I was a vestal virgin, and some mumbo jumbo vows were supposed to turn me into a fabulous lover. I was supposed to be totally submissive and be good at it [sex]." She got her tubes tied when she got divorced.

Judy tells us, "After seven pregnancies, the last one at thirty-seven years old, I decided to have my tubes tied. I knew the church considered it a sin but I decided that God knew me and my needs."

But May, a law librarian in Texas who is a divorced mother of three, tells of her allegiance to the rules. "After freshman year in college I went home . . . and became pregnant, but not really sure how. The nuns had never taught sex education and neither had my parents. I was too naive to know. So, the parish priest, who had known me all my life, wanted to perform the marriage. No way. The young man I was marrying wasn't Catholic and I knew the priest and he would clash, so we were married by a JP [justice of the peace]. Because my religion meant so much to me we were married the following summer, after our son's birth, in a quiet ceremony by a younger priest. My husband didn't agree to follow the church's teaching on birth control, but I wanted to. I had three children in five years, no insurance on the first two, who came thirteen months apart. Got the picture? Hell. Bad. Horrible. The church said I couldn't take the pill. I was going to have a baby a year if I didn't though."

Glenna says, "As a young wife, I had five pregnancies in five years of marriage, resulting in four children. After the birth of my fourth child (whose delivery was difficult because, in the words of my obstetrician, my uterus was 'tired') some progressive young priests were beginning to give permission to use the 'pill.' It was fortunate that, at some point in my religious education, I had been told that if one could get even one priest to declare an act acceptable, it was. Had it not been for this bit of information, gratefully remembered, I wonder how many more children my guilt-ridden body would have produced and what further damage would have been done to our lives." To illustrate her statement, she adds a humorous anecdote about her husband's reaction to a titillating sermon: "I recall one particularly explicit sermon from the pastor of our town's university parish in which he [the priest] described in great detail just what unmarried couples were not allowed to do, with such vigor (and, I later suspected, enjoyment) that my husband . . . declared that he had enjoyed it so much that he planned to go back to the next mass and hear it again."

Some of the women, still wanting to "do it right," went to the church for permission to use birth control. This is seldom granted, and only in extreme situations.

Carmen of Alaska went with her husband to see their priest. "This was a couple of weeks after our first son was born, and I wanted to know if the church would approve our use of 'the pill.' . . . We told him we just couldn't have another baby at this time and would we have the church's permission to use the pill. He said no. To use the rhythm method. . . . It wasn't but a short while, maybe a month or more, before I didn't go to church anymore. The first Sunday I missed church, I thought lightning would surely strike me down." As other women in her situation also realized, Carmen was not struck by lightning when she quit the church. But so strong and thorough is the church's teaching that more than one woman expressed having had the same fear, but did not ask for permission.

Cecile, now sixty-nine and of California, needed a hysterectomy while in her forties, but decided not to ask for permission, standard practice at the time. "Hysterectomies were not accepted by the church at that time except for a very, very good cause. I felt my cause was good enough and so did the doctor. I did not ask holy permission. In 1967 I was relieved of the hemorrhaging and inability to remain on my feet for any length of time. . . . I felt the church had no right over making this discomfort last. Also, without the threat of pregnancy, there would be a freedom of sexual enjoyment. I had used a diaphragm for a few months. . . . It weighed heavily on our . . . conscience. [She confessed to a priest for having used the diaphragm.] I received absolution."

Debbie, the military administrator from Washington state, says, "When I was married for the second time and had my only child, at age thirty, a daughter, I was in for a rude shock. I could only have a baby through C-section, and that one nearly cost me and my child our lives. Up to that time I had felt a little guilty about birth control. After the horror of that experience, nothing could convince me that birth control was wrong." Once again, the reality of life overrode the intangible, and useless, church teaching.

Katrina of Illinois has "never agreed with the church on birth control. I resented having to lie when I got married, for fear of being denied a church wedding if I admitted [to the interviewing priest] that I was already on the pill! I don't feel God ever meant us to just keep on having children we couldn't take care of! He gave us common sense—let us figure out how many children we can afford and want to have! I resent a church that sees fit to pry into the most intimate details of my life and dictate how I ought to be. I am an adult, and I want to be treated as one."

Yet some of the women had mothers who taught them to think and decide for themselves. Kathleen had "a very strong mother. . . . When we discussed sex and children, her philosophy was 'have as many as you can afford, not how many the church tells you to have.' She felt that birth control was necessary and her main theme to me was 'save yourself for marriage, but, if you must do it before, be sure you're protected as your life is on the line.' "

Victoria credits her Italian heritage for a healthy attitude about the church. She knew that her Catholic parents "practiced birth control, and that some of the women [in my family] had had abortions. . . . What was said and what was done were two different things, and no guilt seemed to be felt about this. . . . Italians ignore what they see as nonsense."

Some of the women, still taking their early lessons to heart, carry a burden of disapproval for stepping outside the church's guidelines. One of the gay women to answer the survey, Linda, says, "I would love to be able to be a good Catholic. Now, at age twenty, according to the church, I should be excommunicated for being a [gay] human being." Louise, a single twenty-four-year-old marketing specialist in Boston, had an abortion while in college. She says with some pain that because of this "I am a failed Catholic . . . in my eyes and in [those of] the church." She feels she cannot measure up to the standards set for her so long ago. More shrapnel.

The underlying desire to succeed at being a good Catholic is still strong with some of these women. It might be comforting for them to hear Dusty: "When some woman in Massachusetts [it was actually Rhode Island, and it was MaryAnn Sorrentino] got excommunicated for being pro-choice [she was the Executive Director of Planned Parenthood in Rhode Island at the time], our priest had a sermon about how excommunication went against Christ's teachings—not the other way around. I silently cheered. He made so much sense." One wonders if this man is still a priest.

One Woman Speaks

Myra "was angry when I was told, when I had a stillborn baby, that she wouldn't go to heaven, that she would be in a 'limbo.' I couldn't accept that."

Neither could Maggie. Maggie, if you recall, is fifty-six, a homemaker and artist who has four grown children, and who lives in South Dakota. Among the most touching responses to the question about sexuality and birth control was the one from Maggie. Because what she says is so powerful, I am taking the following space to include most of her comments. It is a fitting end to this chapter. It speaks for itself.

"I have had ten pregnancies in my thirty-seven years of marriage and only have four living (and grown) children. I had an RH problem, lost two babies within a couple of days of birth, had one stillbirth and three miscarriages. And yes, I am still angry! Or maybe, that should be 'finally' angry. . . .

"After I left home and became sexually active . . . I became pregnant. Sex doesn't mean you are smart enough to protect yourself or that you even enjoyed it. After I got married I gave myself permission to do that, saying 'if I'm going to suffer for it, I might as well enjoy it.'

"We got married and . . . six months later our first daughter was born. . . . When I was expecting my second child they discovered that I was RH negative. . . .

"Our third child was born two months prematurely and weighed only 2 lbs. 12 oz. This was 1954. She spent two months in the hospital before she came home to stay. The fourth child was jaundiced at birth but otherwise healthy. By the time I was expecting the fifth my antibody level was very high and the doctors were worried. Me? You had sex, you got pregnant, right? Catholics can't use birth control, they can't say no. . . .

"Number five, a girl, died after two days of life and one transfusion. I never got to hold her but the nursing nun held her up once so I could see her. Even now, it enrages me, they could touch her, why not I?

"The sixth was born by Caesarean section after the amniocentesis procedure showed her to be in critical condition. Born on my birthday, she died two days later, on Christmas.

"Our seventh was stillborn. I carried her a month knowing she was dead. The doctors warned me my pregnancy was in trouble. . . . I prayed that it live at least to be baptized. I really expected to die myself and was very depressed. They induced labor in my eighth month. . . . I hemorrhaged in the labor room and the delivery was extremely painful as the placenta had grown to the side of the uterus. . . . I spent the night with a needle in my arm that was excruciatingly painful, mourning my baby, thinking about Jesus on the cross, and longing for oblivion. . . .

"Our babies are buried in three different states and during this time I also had three miscarriages. I think of our family as close and loving but constant worry about pregnancy had a really bad effect on our primary relationship [marriage]. I suffered from depression if I was late with my period, fearing I was pregnant. . . .

". . . At times I felt hatred for my husband. . . . We had sex when my husband wanted it, and when he wanted it we had sex. But who was doing the suffering, whose life was on the line? The feminist saying 'the penis has no conscience' is all too sadly true, but it was his children we lost also. Didn't he feel responsible? Like all too many men he apparently, and I feel with the blessing of the church, considered sex his right and pregnancy my responsibility—in effect, my fault!

"When our fifth child died, he said, 'No more!' He didn't mean it. . . .

"By this time, 1967, great changes were being made. The pill, IUDs, etc. After my stillbirth and my subsequent depression my husband finally went to see the base chaplain . . . [who said that] chaplains had agreed that if a couple had good reason to use birth control they could, and suggested I go on the pill. I could hardly believe it, a priest saying that! Well, a good Catholic confesses doubts, so I went on the pill but I also confessed it and my confessor turned out to be not the liberal-minded chaplain but one of the old school who challenged me with 'the pope hasn't given you permission to use birth control,' to which I replied,

'But Father, I just can't stand to lose another baby.' I got no sympathy and didn't say another word for the entire confession, not even 'Thank you, Father' at the end. I was determined not to give him the pleasure of correcting a sobbing woman. . . .

"Well, I eventually learned the 'confess but don't tell all method' of other Catholics and continued to be one, but on the pill. This was a time when people went to confession in one parish where the priest 'allowed' birth control and to communion at their own if their priest didn't! . . .

"I had a tubal ligation in 1972, the best thing I've ever done for myself. They needed my husband's permission! . . . The church calls it self-mutilation and condemns it along with abortion. Lay Catholics always pick and choose what they condemn or defend. . . .

". . . My religion allowed me to risk my life over and over to try to bring into the world babies who really had little or no chance for life when I already had four children who needed me. No angel from heaven comes down to comfort the motherless or for that matter the mother who has lost her child.

"I feel more sinned against than sinner!"

Today Maggie is a Unitarian Universalist. She brought her husband and children with her to their new church.

5

Useless Dogma

Q. 163: What is meant by the infallibility of the Catholic Church?

Answer: By the infallibility of the Catholic Church is meant that the Church, by the special assistance of the Holy Ghost, cannot err when it teaches or believes a doctrine of faith or morals.

—*The New Baltimore Catechism* (p. 73)

Exercise Question 3.6: James is not a Catholic yet, though he has said he is going to become one. Suddenly he is run over by an automobile. What would you do for him to help him save his soul since he is now badly hurt?

—*The New Baltimore Catechism* (p. 144)

After a lifetime of instruction to turn to the church for help, when many of the women did, they found a closed door. The clergy, if they heard the women's requests for aid or comfort, offered little or no solace, and frequently even damaged them further. Often, the church's cure for the church-given illness of guilt and shame was more of the same.

Betrayal

Karen of Pennsylvania tells an especially poignant story. "When I was nineteen, my eldest brother died. He had a brain tumor, but it was not properly diagnosed until the day before he died. He spent the last two years of his life in insane asylums.

"His death tore my family apart. My mother took it especially hard. She felt guilty for not getting the right kind of medical treatment. I sank into a deep depression. I had literally worshipped my brother.

"Fifteen months after my brother's death, my mother was diagnosed as having the same type of tumor. She had a stroke during surgery, and went into a coma. Nearly out of my mind with grief I turned to the church.

"I explained my situation to the parish priest. (He knew it all anyway as my father was having novenas said for my mother's recovery.) His voice was very soft and sincere. Didn't my brother recently die of the same thing? Yes, he had, I said. And hadn't my brother married a Jewish girl? Yes, he had, I said. Poor Marcy, she felt so bad.

" 'It was obvious,' the priest explained to me, 'that God was punishing' my family for its sins. My brother had died 'because he had married outside the faith.' My mother was dying 'because she allowed it.' They were both going to burn in hell. And he said it so quietly and reasonably.

"I went home and tried to kill myself.

"Now I know that he was a fruitcake, but I've never set foot in a Catholic church again (except for my mother's funeral and my father's funeral). The very idea makes me feel ill."

When Maggie's husband was gravely ill, their church had no contact with them, except "when Ed got home a month later, and our donation cards came in the mail.

"We stopped going to church. I felt guilty at first but also relieved. We had gone too many times looking and longing for some wisdom and support from the man on the altar only to get a sermon on guardian angels."

Sara believes: "The priests lecture rather than truly help people in trouble. There are exceptions but I have not been treated that well by the priests I ran into.

"For instance, my ex-husband and I spoke to a priest to try to save our marriage. We told him our problems, which were many. It was as if he didn't hear a word we said. He said, 'You have no problems. Hold hands and go home; things will be OK.' Is this treating or understanding the human condition? No, the church said we had to stay married no matter what and that's how the priest reacted.

"I finally left that man but because the church hasn't approved the divorce I am not allowed to remarry [in the church]. I have met a man I truly love but the church says, 'Tough, you have to be alone the rest of your life.' Well, I am getting married anyway even if I marry in a civil ceremony. . . . The church has standards no normal person can attain. It fails to take into account that people are human."

Kathleen of Ohio has a similar story. "After my separation from my husband in early 1985, I continued attending church on a weekly basis. In 1986, after the final divorce decree, I began dating a man (whom I am still seeing) and gradually fell away from the church because of its refusal to see me as a person *needing* another life partner. My divorce was caused by my husband's dating another woman when I was eight months pregnant—he decided when I was six months pregnant that we had made a 'mistake' in having a child although she was *planned* and wanted by both of us (after using birth control for twelve years!). Is this *my fault*? Why am I condemned to live the rest of my life alone because someone else decided *they* wanted a divorce!"

Lily of Missouri remembers incidents that told her the church, in a variety of locations around the country, just was not there for her when she turned to it for help: "The time my son was dying and the priest couldn't come because he had a luncheon engagement. . . . The time I was alone and pregnant and considering abortion and suicide and the priest couldn't talk with me because he had a golf date. . . . The time the Franciscan head of a Catholic college put the moves on me when I was a student. . . . The sister . . . who used cleanser on a paper towel to rub my mouth when I had on lipstick in the eighth grade. . . . Another sister . . . who sent me home . . . on the city bus when I had started menstruating and had bled through my clothes and I did not have any idea of what was happening to me. I was *terrified*. . . . The priest who threw me out of class and threatened to prevent me from graduating high school because I asked for more . . . information about the Inquisition."

Joan, the computer operator and mother of two in Ohio, was a depressed teenager whose parents could not afford counseling, so she went to her local pastor. "I asked his advice, when everything was so overwhelming to me. He told me to say three Hail Marys and everything would be fine. It wasn't, and I was greatly disturbed by his cold response. Some months later, the pastor dropped dead with a heart attack, and I felt relieved. The man would no longer be around, giving such empty advice."

Natalie's sister was confronted by "the priest who told her, in front of her son, that she would risk hell and jeopardize her immortal soul if she remarried" after her divorce. She did so anyway.

During Evelyn's parents' divorce, "this very difficult time, I turned to my church. It was the sun my life had revolved around.

I went to it for help, for love, for all the things it had promised to be.

"But there was no help. Parochial school became a prison. I felt isolated. I no longer fit in. Parochial school was the place that 'good' Catholic families sent their children. 'Good' families do not divorce.

"I became an embarrassing question, a mistake the church had no answer for. Although I had always been quiet and a good student, the teachers' attitudes towards me changed. I was 'cracked down on' and treated as if a discipline problem. I was no longer welcome in some of my classmates' homes. . . .

"During this time my mother went to the priest for guidance, but he could give neither condolence nor help. . . . He told her blankly that she could not divorce my father (who already had plans to remarry) and if she did she could never remarry. . . . My mother chose to divorce, which I think was the least painful for her under the circumstances. But through all the loneliness and pain, the church was not there" for her. Evelyn left the church shortly after and has never returned.

Irene, the payroll clerk from California, describes herself as having been a promiscuous teenager, so she turned to the church for guidance. "All these years of participation in Catholic schools and Catholic church. All I wanted was direction, encouragement, love—all I ever got was hell and damnation. There was not a single nun or priest who paid attention to any of my needs."

MaryAnn remembers "being very angry when, as a teenager, I found myself in a vicious cycle of confessing masturbation over and over again. I became very impatient with this process, longing for power or deliverance if this was indeed an evil practice. I finally realized that if this were truly a helpful or charitable institution, they would have recommended I see a doctor if I was really oversexed or they would have realized that such thoughts and practices were very normal and natural and nothing to be ashamed of, instead of this interminable, futile, and pointless procedure of weekly confession with no change."

One of the respondents notes "that all the people called 'saints' by the Roman Catholics are people who did things that are forbidden by that church. We were told we couldn't (shouldn't) try to talk directly to God—saints did. We were told never to meditate to any depth—saints did. . . . So, if we did those actions and were *sinners*, please explain how *they* can be '*saints*'? Confusion!" She adds: "How can the church encourage us to use our minds to develop science and medicine, but not use birth control?"

Several would agree with Carmen who observes, "I have to chuckle to myself when I think of how suddenly [after Vatican II] it was no longer a mortal sin to eat meat on Fridays, and you wouldn't have to burn in hell, whereas before they lifted the ban, the church claims you would have had to burn." Terry questions the change in rules. "If it used to be unacceptable in God's eyes for a female to attend church without a hat or head covering of some type, how could this change? Did God get glasses? . . . All those years of praying to several of the saints were in vain. We were then told that some of the saints had been cancelled. . . . I once called the church with a marital problem and the nun that I spoke to suggested divorce."

But Cathy "absorbed and became what I was taught. I was sincere and believed totally. I trusted. I look back on nights of guilt and tears because I forgot to confess a 'sin,' took a bite of a hot dog on a Friday, or drank something less than one hour before communion." She feels "betrayal by the church. . . . How can the church change policies that were once sins? How can they say to me, 'Thank you very much—you suffered, but, well, look—now you don't have to do that anymore—*we* have "grown." ' I feel totally invalidated!"

Margo agrees. The "hierarchy never apologized [for pre-Vatican II teachings]. [They never said] 'we screwed up—we are sorry all of you who learned you were bad—we made a mistake; God is good.' They never admitted they screwed up." For some of the women here, a confession on the part of the church would be a refreshing change.

Louise tells of her mother, who "is a good Catholic. [But when she was divorced years ago] she was excommunicated. She could not receive communion. They gave her guilt, and she was made to feel apart. My mother went to a priest but wouldn't apologize and wouldn't swear to never divorce again, so they wouldn't let her back in. She said if she'd apologized, it would give them what they wanted, and she couldn't do that. She is still excommunicated." She says it is this hostility toward her mother that has pushed her away from the church.

Kathleen's grandmother went to the Catholic church for help when her husband was killed in an accident. "She was told by the priest to 'trust in the Lord.' . . . In despair—she had no skills, she was an immigrant who didn't speak any English—she visited a Protestant church. The minister took up a collection of money, food, and clothing and helped the family out for a few years until they were able to support themselves. I guess Catholics trust in the Lord and Protestants help other humans in need!"

Victoria says the thing that makes her the angriest is "the guilt that the church has successfully instilled, especially for the weird—and sick—idea that Christ died for my sins or anyone's sins. Because neither I or anyone I know has done anything *that* bad, that justifies this sick thing of this man being . . . nailed to a cross and bleeding to death. If he feels he has to do that for me, I'm sorry, that's a terribly misplaced burden. I didn't do anything that bad!"

Abby hates that the church "is continuing to perpetuate myths and traditions that are intolerant and hurting other people, and keeping people from feeling their potential as human beings. They do this under the guise of some kind of truth or reality. It's all a myth."

"What I have come to realize," Loretta says, ". . . is that my anger is toward the concept of God that I formed as a child, and at the system which allowed that to happen. . . . Unfortunately, the legacy they passed along was a very sick philosophy of life."

As to how the church influences dysfunctional families, Lily offers: "My mother, trained by the sisters . . . to despise her own sexuality, was shocked and offended to produce another flawed being—a replica of herself—a female. She [beat] . . . me behind the knees with sticks. It ended when I was fourteen and took away from her the chunk of kindling she was going to hit me with. She never told me *anything* about being a woman [menstruation, etc.]. The church had stopped her up forever. The Catholic church is a bloated monstrosity, feeding on the broken hearts and spirits of women."

Hypocrisy

Perhaps less personal, but about as offensive, an affront is what the women detail as the church's ability to preach one thing while doing the opposite.

Is Roman Catholicism a religion or a business? Linda of Texas refers to it as "Roman Catholicism, Inc.," and several of the women question its priorities.

Several would agree with Beth of Massachusetts who says, "What really annoys me is the church's vast wealth. They own too much gold. Their money would be better used in youth programs, and to better the people in the world." Sara asks, "Let's face it, if people truly looked at the church, . . . its mafia connections, etc., who would believe a word they said? . . . They teach poverty while they have a seat on the New York Stock Exchange. They preach love but look down upon anyone that's not Catholic. They preach equality but treat women like dirt. I can't stand hypocrisy; the church is full of it!" And Victoria: "The distance of the church from real social problems" makes her angry. "Look at Spain, where the richness of the church is surrounded by poverty."

Barbara of Texas resents how "they [the church] get involved politically, swaying votes, yet they don't pay taxes. They own land, have lots of resources and money. This annoys me. Do they want to get into politics? Then tax them."

Debbie noticed, "If daddy was rich and a contributing member of the church, his son/daughter was the prize student [to the nuns]. Everyone else got yelled at and . . . abused verbally."

None of this is new, of course. Victoria, again, remembers, "My father was a sexton [custodian] and cook at the local church rectory during the Depression, in the 1930s and into the 1940s. He took home the priests' cast-off silk pajamas. . . . The priests ate very well. My father shopped for their food. He bought and served too much so that he could take the leftovers home. Therefore he had a cynicism about the priesthood, which was 'in the air' at my home." She says there's an old Italian saying, "strotsa priete," that describes a meal so big "it would choke even a priest." Church riches were known in the old country, and were noted by the people in another saying that compares levels of wealth, "he's as rich as the pope." She adds, "my father also knew of the affairs the priests were having with women in the parish."

"Collecting money during the course of the mass, especially

during prayers, has to be one of the crassest, most avaricious acts perpetuated by the church," Polly contends. "Talk about denigrating the sanctity of worship!"

One woman says, "The part that makes me angriest is the exploitation of human beings in the name of God for some man-made power structure. . . . It wasn't until . . . I was around twenty-one, that I actually broke with the church and understood that the only doctrines they were interested in maintaining were the politically advantageous ones."

Martha supports that belief. She learned, through her early studies to become a nun, that "God wasn't behind a lot of it, no matter how often His will was invoked in support" of the various church-sponsored activities.

One says her eyes were opened when the Catholic school officials would not let her child attend the school "because we had no record of weekly contributions. I hadn't been going to church [because she had several young children]. For the first time, I saw through that Roman collar and what I saw wasn't very pretty. How could I have had such faith in what I now saw as a complete fraud. These weren't God's representatives on earth. They were just human like me and from what I saw, not much better."

Many of the women would agree that the Roman Catholic church is a business masquerading as a religion. The pope is the Chief Executive Officer, the curia is the board of directors, the cardinals are the regional vice presidents, the priests are the sales managers. The laypeople are the customers. For a long time the Catholic church has acted as if it had no competition. But they have been losing sales managers (priests) to scandal and to secular life, and now customers are being lured away by the competition, including evangelicals or Protestants or New Age groups, who offer a better product in the eyes of the customers.

So the CEO reacts the only way he knows how: he roars with anger, he issues directives, he clamps down on dissent. Onlookers say he must be losing control, must be feeling panic, to resort to such outdated methods. The company sure isn't what it used to be, they observe. It has to change, but with him in charge, it won't. And it still may not change with a new CEO.

The church-as-a-business model takes on credibility when the women talk about obtaining an annulment, and the fee involved. Katrina of Illinois "really got turned off when I learned what it takes to get an annulment in the church—knowing the right person, and having the right amount of cash. I found this out when a friend, who got a divorce after her husband deserted her, wanted to get an annulment to stay in good grace with the church. It came down to money and the right person—so much for a holy sacrament!" Bobbie agrees. "I saw the annulment my cousin had to go through and was vastly surprised. The intimate, exploiting questions you must answer to the priest are uncalled for. I feel, you answer only to God.

"I was extremely appalled at the annulment questionnaire and the exorbitant price to get one—if it goes through—after the hours of testimony you must give. It is like you are in a courtroom telling all about your intimate life. God knows what you do. No one else should. This is what totally turned me off from the Catholic church."

Dusty, the writer from Pennsylvania, tells us about the annulment process itself. "My divorce in 1977 first brought me to the ranks of the damned. During the separation a priest I thought I'd trusted lectured me for being selfish and for not doing my wifely duty. I never went back to him.

"When I got the forms to complete for an annulment, I couldn't do it. How could I expose my innermost feelings, disappointments, shames, etc., to a bunch of men who had never been married, so they could sit in judgment of me and decide whether or not I had really been married?

"The whole thing made no sense to me. . . . If I'd committed a murder, all I'd have to do to get back on the heaven list was make a 'good confession'—in private. . . . But because I had been dumb enough to marry the wrong person when I was nineteen, I had to be put through this horrible procedure. Forget it!"

What about the church's stand on birth control: does it say that the church really loves children?

Candy, the thirty-six-year-old military officer, notes that, "The Catholic church . . . preaches love, forgiveness, and charity but yet it remains cold and aloof to many of its own children. I have friends who are single mothers and who have been severely reprimanded by their priest. I also have friends who are gay and have been shunned by the church. What kind of 'fatherly love' is this?" She adds, "When Jesus loved children so unconditionally how can a church find so much fault in our innocence?!"

Another agrees, saying, "Given its blind stand on birth control, the Catholic church's position on abortion was to be expected. But I have observed nothing that leads me to believe that these attitudes are prompted by love of children. A crying child was never welcome in our church, and I doubt that any priest could have endured for more than one day the family environment to which most of their parishioners were subjected. Most of the large Catholic families in our town lived on the edge of poverty. The priests' quarters were quite comfortable." And another: "The church says, 'Have them but keep them quiet!' " She also recalls a nephew's christening, "during which the priest was insulting to non-Catholics," some of whom were in attendance.

Abby believes that the church is not children-oriented. "I don't think the church has ever really cared a whole lot about kids. The whole church is based on dogma that's not healthy for kids—things like guilt, suffering, pain; on higher places in heaven being [awarded] based on how much pain you can endure—these are really not kid-oriented kinds of messages. The whole church is not a child-healthy-oriented institution. So if a few kids get sexually abused, you just cover that up, try to make excuses, try to blame your victims, try to get the focus off where the blame really belongs."

Maggie adds her voice to those who would point out this dichotomy between doctrine and practice. "One [military chaplain priest] I remember must have not liked children. If a child cried or let out any noise during mass he would stop whatever he was saying or doing until the church became deathly silent and the offending parents exited with their offspring."

The church's history is questionable in its support of Christ's teachings on peace. Abby observes, "It's always surprised me that the church spends a lot of time giving members information how they should vote, etc., but have not taken an active stance against war. For example, during the Vietnam War, the church officials were quiet."

One of the women, Lily, belonged to a church that enthusiastically supported the war in Vietnam, which caused her to doubt the veracity of church teachings. "My parish in Illinois held a carnival. One of the 'games' was 'Viet Cong Bombing Raid.' Children were to drop 'bombs' on little villages to see how much they could destroy, to obtain prizes. My outrage was met with accusations that I was 'disturbed' and a 'troublemaker.' The pastor also preached regularly that there was no salvation outside the Catholic church. The bishop refused to do anything about either of these travesties. This was 1965." And her handicapped son was expelled from a Catholic grade school in 1967 "when it became known through a newspaper article that I had attended the New Politics convention in Chicago that summer as a delegate from the local anti-war committee on Vietnam." She says she "came to see that these incidents were not isolated, bizarre events . . . but instead were part and parcel, warp and woof of what the church *was*. This was its nature: degrade into hopelessness sufficient that the cross would be embraced and all expectations would be focused on death."

Adrianne saw "on CNN . . . a reporter was interviewing a Catholic church scholar about the authenticity of an apparition of the Virgin that had been appearing regularly somewhere in France. This particular scholar maintained a view, that was supposed to be held by the church, that this appearance was a hoax perpetrated by Satan. One of the reasons for this conclusion was that the vision told people that the church should, as a policy, promote peace. The scholar said that it was not the church's job to spread peace. Leaving us to conclude that it was Satan's job, I suppose."

One woman points to "the Crusades, the Inquisition, the witch burnings, participation in violence against indigenous people by missionaries, anti-Semitism" as actions by the church that go against its claim to be a source of peace for its followers. Another comments, "How could the pope allow Jews to be exterminated during World War II? (He didn't want to get involved!) . . . How can the pope/church have so much wealth, and yet people die daily of starvation and the atrocities of war? (It's much easier to preach peace than to live peacefully!)"

On one of the church's favorite subjects, sex, the women call the church on its own "sins."

Nan says, "We . . . had a priest who had a young live-in housekeeper. They had four children. Every time they had one, he got up in the pulpit and thanked God for allowing them to *adopt* another child. I can't see how the rest of the congregation could stay there. I left!"

Kelly of Illinois adds, "I saw Phil Donahue's show on pederast priests and it was very interesting. It would seem that more than a few sexually disturbed people are drawn to the priesthood because they know the bishops will protect them." The Father Porter case in Massachusetts and Minnesota has brought this problem into the national spotlight. "Another show mentioned . . . that a large majority of people who are attracted to the ministry are themselves imbued with a deep sexual shame. I don't need someone with a weak moral character being held up to me as a god. It was also pointed out on the Donahue show by a psychiatrist who treats these pederast priests that they all told him the same thing: that they had gone through four years of seminary, and human sexuality was never mentioned."

Margo is still "angry at the way the priests are protected by the hierarchy. . . . A lot of priests were seductive. And a lot of the priests I knew have left, married, and now have kids. . . . Priests are just human beings." Another woman adds, "I have been subject to attempts to seduce me by priests." And another: "While in a state of shock after the death of my husband, I became involved with a Catholic priest—his sexual advances became too much for me. I then moved out of the city."

Abby notes an irony: "[As Boston's] Cardinal Law's first priority as a new cardinal . . . he made it very clear that he'd fight against abortion . . . not segregation. . . . This is a man who knows nothing about marriage."

Connie, the sixty-three-year-old nurse in Florida, wryly notes, "My mother can't understand where [Father] Andrew Greeley gets all his sex info for his books. Priests aren't supposed to know all that stuff." Her mother is not the only one who wonders.

Myra "realized that priests and nuns were having affairs with each other in the 1970s. I was angry that they preached one thing and did another. I believe that many Catholic priests are sick men. Why would any normal man (or woman) these days choose celibacy? Catholic priests are now dying of AIDS! Catholic priests are . . . accused of molesting boys! There are treatment centers for Catholic priests. . . . What does all this say for the Catholic church?"

In the 1990s, the media has exploded with stories of sexual abuse of children by priests. In some cases, the abuse took place in the 1950s and 1960s, and was only recently brought to light by men and women who could no longer keep their past to themselves.

Hardly a week passes without there being a story about alleged abuse, either committed long ago or more recently, by priests, bishops, and even cardinals. As of this writing, even jokes, which are a measure of how deep an issue has permeated our culture, are circulating. One was reported by one of the women surveyed here, Hillary, about a young man reaching a career decision: "Hey, Mom! You don't have to fix me up with any more pretty, pious, single daughters of your friends! I'm going to join the priesthood!" Even the best public relations firm does not have enough fingers to plug all the holes in the dike that's seemingly bursting with these reports.

Martha does not see this news as something the church is doing to "confess its sins," but rather as "the courage of the priests' victims in pursuing justice . . . [as] the real driving force here." She then tells a chilling story about a priest she knew while she was studying to become a nun. "Dan (not his real name) was transferred from a rural parish in a neighboring state to our inner city parish. Over time, Dan revealed to me the true nature of his placement at our church. He was in trouble with the law: during his tenure as pastor at his last parish, he'd seduced a number of young adolescent boys, and one of these boys had confessed to his mother what Father Dan had done to him. Were it not for the fact that he was a 'man of the cloth,' Dan told me, he'd be in jail that very minute. Dan's bishop had 'rescued' him and arranged for Dan to come to our parish, where he wouldn't be recognized. Apparently the hope was that the statute of limitations on pressing charges would cause the case to expire before the young boy's family chose to act.

"I knew that Dan was receiving psychiatric services several times a week. We talked about what had happened to him and how he was progressing; and I asked him why he hadn't sought out adult companionship [at his old parish] instead, if he had to break his promise of celibacy at all. . . . 'There weren't any gay men around,' he answered. 'They all come to the cities to look for partners.' I could never detect any remorse in Dan, any sense of wrongdoing in his pursuing underage males to satisfy his needs—just an attitude of hurt, of being misunderstood. When I asked Dan what celibacy meant to him, he replied that it barred him from having sexual relations with a *woman*. . . .

"Later, after I left the convent, I learned from someone who knew Dan and his situation that he admitted to cruising the city parks, looking for anonymous sexual partners. I happen to know that Dan is no longer a priest. Only God knows how many 'Dans' there have been, and still are, out there."

Martha goes on to theorize that "the hierarchy of the church, in protecting the sex offenders among its clergy, was [supposedly] taking care of its own while trying to protect the faith of the laity. But are not the laity also the church's 'own'?" The issue Martha raises—what is a church but its people?—is explored more extensively in another chapter. "To send known pedophiles back into parish work in new locations, filled with unsuspecting parishioners and a fresh crop of children to prey on, is unconscionable." She maintains that, "For centuries the church has been in a state of denial about its own humanity, its own sinfulness.

If the church can bring itself to admit it can be and has been wrong, it could move beyond its alienation to a greater wholeness and holiness."

Cyndy follows the same theme. "The church has always ignored and refused to deal with the fact that we are all sexual beings with sexual urges. That ignorance allowed the unspeakable acts of men with power over women and children. The church's teachings caused the situation; such perversions proliferate when sexual urges are surpressed and ignored."

These abuses show, Cyndy continues, "that the lives priests are expected to lead are unreasonable and that this leads to repressed sexuality, which in turn leads to immoral behavior. . . . It reinforces the need for reformation. . . . I think it is natural that these problems would arise sooner or later, because the theology sets up the environment for such occurrences."

Kathleen says that, "The men who are attracted [to the priesthood] 'act out' sexually with children, and the church will be judged harshly because they choose to cover it up and deny it. These sexual abuses make a mockery of the priesthood and the faith!"

Abby adds, "I've always wondered why an individual would choose a profession that takes such an important piece of your life away from you, and calls this good, that piece being loving relationships and sexual relationships. Who would be drawn to that kind of profession? I think we really have to question that. I'm really not surprised that a lot of these men . . . are the kinds of people with power problems. Child abuse goes hand in hand with major-league power problems. I wonder how many others were abused by priests sexually and emotionally and in other ways who will never come forward."

Donna of Minnesota wonders "why men enter the priesthood. Do they actually have a so-called calling or do they have something else going on inside? What was their upbringing like?" She says, "Priests are being deprived of one of life's greatest pleasures, a sexual relationship. The church again is casting out women. It appears that priests felt it okay to abuse children, but women were off limits."

Margo agrees that the church maintained a cover-up of these abusive priests. "The church did a good job of covering up the abusers, sad but true. I personally know an ex-priest who was molested [by another priest] while he was [still] a priest. The abusers . . . have their own twisted morals they live by. I am glad it's 'out.' Thank *God*! These men are sick."

Abby sees the church's self-protection as their paramount concern. "You protect the hierarchy of the church at any cost. It didn't—and probably still doesn't—make a whole lot of dif-ference [to the church] who gets hurt in that process. Catholic history . . . shows that has always been the Number One issue for the Catholic church: maintaining the institution. And you do that, at whatever cost you have to, and it if means protecting child-molesting priests, you do that; if it means lying, you do that; if it means changing midstream some kind of edict that you had all along because [otherwise] you're losing money . . . you do what you have to do to maintain this institution."

Abby reveals a great respect for the survivors of these abuses: "Had they not been strong enough, and had these times not been times when we've grown to recognize what child abuse is all about, if they hadn't come forward and hadn't pushed, the church would still be hiding these things. . . . I feel an absolute respect and absolute admiration for these people who have come forward to really call these things what they are and are trying to stop this [abuse]."

But even now, the church pours salt into the wounds of these victims. In the famous case of Father James Porter of Attleboro,

Massachusetts, and four other locations where the priest has been accused of sexually abusing boys and girls during the 1960s and 1970s, a priest who was witness to some of the abuse was recently promoted by the church. This priest actually walked in on Porter as he was molesting children, allegedly retreating from the room and closing the door so that Porter would not be interrupted. In 1993, even after the accusations against Porter were made, the archdiocese "elevated to monsignor" the priest who apparently saw the abuse, and the bishop was quoted as saying that while the priest's accusers say he did nothing to stop what was going on, and that they are probably well-meaning, "their memories 'may have been confused' by the trauma of what had happened to them" (*Boston Globe*, March 15, 1993).

And in December of 1993, after Porter pleaded guilty and was sentenced to 18 to 20 years in prison, the archdiocese ran a cartoon in the *Anchor*, the diocese's weekly paper. It depicted the Porter victims as coming forward only for money to be gained by suing the church. "It showed a [psychiatrist's] receptionist asking a client, 'How much abuse can you afford to remember?' " A few days later, after several of the Porter abuse survivors protested the cartoon, Bishop Sean O'Malley called it "inappropriate and insensitive" (*Patriot Ledger*, December 15, 1993). But the damage was already done.

Abby concludes by saying, "I think the cartoon tells it all; it really speaks to me about what the church is *still* all about when it comes to these issues. I don't think the church really gives a damn about the survivors [of this abuse]. I don't think they give a damn about the individual people whose lives are affected by these men."

Perhaps the Catholic church becomes a victim of its declaration of infallibility by disappointing those who see church leaders as simply human.

Blind Faith

The women maintain that the methods used to teach them their faith gave them no tools for real life, for figuring things out in a crisis.

Janet of Vermont says, "You don't ask questions [in the Catholic church]. You learn just dogma, rote learning. We weren't allowed to read the Bible because we might misinterpret it. If you had any questions? The church could answer them. That's all you needed was the dogma—anything beyond that was wrong. If you didn't let the church answer your questions and tried to do it on your own, you were bad and you felt guilty. It's a vicious circle."

Kelly says, "There was no encouragement to think independently. Blind faith was what was encouraged. No freedom to think for yourself. You could only find the correct answer that they sought. The catechism was learned by rote and so was everything else. . . .

"The only comparable experience I can imagine would be a religious cult. That's what I think of the Catholic religion. The constant brainwashing, the chanting, the incense, the total immersion of life after school. (We had to watch TV shows that they wanted us to). They controlled all our waking moments. It was definitely thought control at its worst. Some of the memorable phrases I recall are 'the burning fires of hell'; 'The Protestants . . . are going to put your back up against a wall and test your faith'; 'If you just think of sin, you're guilty of it.' I could go on for ten years. Movies you couldn't see. Records you couldn't listen to because they were 'occasions of sin.' Once, in about third grade, a nun called us (girls only) into the room and informed us that under no conditions were we ever to listen to a song called 'Make Yourself Comfortable.' I think it was by Sarah Vaughan. I did listen to it knowing all the while I was a sinner, but I couldn't figure out what was so inherently wrong with making yourself 'comfortable.' "

Martha, who studied to be a nun, remembers that in college she realized she wasn't a bad person. "I realized how afraid and guilt-ridden I was and had been for years. I began to get very angry at what and how I had been taught about my faith—the quality of the message delivered over the years from the pulpit. 'They teach as dogmas mere human precepts' (Mark 7:7)." She asks, "Do they really expect me to believe: that all those loaves and fishes multiplied? that Jesus walked on the water? that God loves me unconditionally, when there are all these rules and regulations I have to obey to stay in His good graces?"

Within the church, one certainly cannot question canon. When Martha was in convent school, she had this experience: "One day in our formal group instruction, we discussed Mary's 'fiat,' her unequivocal yes to the archangel announcing that she would bear the son of God. My old problem with Mary resurfaced as a question: 'If Mary really had a choice, she could have said "no" to God, right? If there's a "yes," there has to be a "no." ' If silence were ice, that room could have sunk the *Titanic*. The . . . directors clenched their jaws and stared angrily, while my fellow initiates looked horrified. I stammered something conciliatory and abandoned the subject." It was a fascinating question that was left unexplored that day.

Another woman says the church tells us "that we are supposed to shut off our brains and accept boring masses, social inequity in the church, and pat answers to complex concerns. I feel rage when I think of how passive and patient my faith taught me to be." Another agrees: "The church's method of teaching its beliefs . . . imprisons its members, and tries to manipulate their minds. Catholicism has some cult-like qualities in that it tries to force its beliefs on non-Catholic society."

Nicole of California asks, "It has . . . been noted . . . that certain 'books' [of the Bible] were removed by a council of the church. To hide what?"

"I feel that my religious education was a rip-off," says Polly. "I learned nothing of the church's history, only dogma and cant. I learned nothing of other religions, only that Catholics believed 'correctly'; there was no room for discussion or diversity. It wasn't until I was in college that I learned anything about the history of Catholicism and some of its philosophy of religion. I strongly feel that I learned little of value. Certainly, the foundation of Christian ethics and morality was there, and this is of some value, but the fact that these values are taught through guilt and the attitude that if you do good works, you will go to heaven—rather than teaching that good works should be done joyfully, without the promise of reward—just isn't kosher. Stick-and-carrot/reward-and-punishment, etc., just doesn't cut it in my book."

Patricia of New York remembers that "we recited Rosaries as a family, went to mass every holy day of obligation, attended CCD classes, and bingo. We had a crucifix on every wall, and paintings of Mary and Joseph over my parents' bed, with palms from Palm Sunday tucked behind the frames. On vacations, when we four children would fight, my father would make us recite Rosaries in the car. There were St. Christopher and St. Anthony medals in every car. Statuettes of Mary guarded the stove and an Infant of Prague watched over the stairs. . . .

"I first doubted the Catholic church when I started confirmation class. . . . I learned nothing but dread. Each week we were handed Xerox copies of dogma and rules. The following week, some unlucky sinner would be led to the front of the class and interrogated, usually until tears. We were not to understand how the teachings fit together, or the history of the beliefs, we were just to memorize them. The only goal seemed to be to impress the bishop—for Sister told us we would burn in hell if we embarrassed her by not knowing the answers. I couldn't stand such useless memorization." And Patricia recalls, with some humor, "My earliest memory is of Easter mass. I was holding a candle and caught my hair on fire. I guess I should have known I was doomed."

Maggie says, "I grew up in a rural area. . . . Every Saturday during the summer our parish priest taught catechism class. I dreaded it and we had to know the answer word for word. Father often ridiculed my older cousin, a boy, by comparing him to a parrot. I worried constantly that I would forget part of an answer and become the recipient of his sarcasm." She also describes herself then as someone who "never questioned the church and defended it to all detractors. . . . Of course the pope is infallible! I gazed at the Eucharist when it was raised during mass and longed to really see Christ. I was careful not to let the host touch my teeth and tried to pry it free from the roof of my mouth as unobtrusively and respectfully as possible."

Glenna says, "As a child I was accepting of my subordinate position in a male-dominated church that considered women unfit for total participation in the rites of the religion. I am still puzzled and a little embarrassed that I was so completely indoctrinated during my eight years of Catholic school. By the time I was of child-bearing age I firmly believed that . . . I was a member of the one true faith; . . . virginity, especially in women, was a mark of true sainthood (A careful distinction was made between the female saints who were virgins and those who were not. I was especially fascinated by the often-told story of Blessed Maria Goretti, a comparatively contemporary young girl who supposedly died rather than lose her virtue); . . . almost anything was permissible under the right circumstances, but not even to save a woman's life might one use artificial means of contraception; and . . . divorce and remarriage were absolutely forbidden, no matter how desperate the circumstances. (There were always stories, of course, of people—usually with some influence—who managed to get an annulment, but I preferred not to believe these)."

Martha adds, "Attending the usual Confraternity of Christian Doctrine [CCD, or Sunday school] classes, I used those catechisms with the cheerful, brightly colored illustrations and memorized the expected answers to the predictable questions. But I knew that was kid stuff. I knew where the real message came from— I knew threats when I heard them."

One woman notes, "I understood it was a 'mortal sin' to question any of the teachings of the church so I never did. That is not in my essential nature, to let other people do the thinking for me. I now believe that it is quite strange not to have questions about theology, and to believe something without questioning it would be not to exercise the 'free will' given each of us, that the nuns told us so much about."

Some did question, and realized that after all, they *didn't* believe. Susan's son "was three years old. I hadn't taught him yet about God or about the church, despite pressure from my mother [to do so]." Her son asked her about words to a prayer that didn't make sense to him. When she looked at it, it didn't make sense to her, either. "I looked again at Catholic tenets and realized I didn't believe *any* of it, except for the kindness of Mary. The wisdom of my child got me to think. I stopped going to church at this point."

Darla and her husband studied religion together early in their marriage. "The more my husband and I studied, the more questions we had to ask, the more the answers did not satisfy. In the end, we had to quit the church as a matter of conscience because we couldn't believe what they taught, so how could we stay!"

The church has taught its followers that they are superior, which today these women do not believe. Perhaps it was taught as a way of giving some sort of justification for the pain and suffering in being a "good" Catholic.

Natalie, the homemaker and mother of three in Massachusetts, will "never forget sitting in my . . . Sunday school class, listening to my teacher explain how to correctly form our hands to pray. 'Point them straight to heaven like a strong steeple,' she would say. 'Not like this (and she would grasp her hands together) like an old, crumbled-down Protestant church.' . . . We were made to feel superior as Catholics, like the 'chosen ones.' My husband, raised as a Protestant, supports that. He always said, 'They acted as if they were better than the Protestant kids and the priests encouraged that.' Frankly I was always jealous of the Protestants because they could skip church without fear of going to hell." This derision of non-Catholics was common and may still be.

Another woman tells us "one thing that angers me about the church is the way the priests say that Catholic . . . school teachers are more dedicated than public school teachers (usually because they work for lower wages). *Bulloney!* Most Catholic school teachers jump to the public school system as soon as an opening appears, or they may be *retired* public school teachers trying to supplement their income. Why can't they [the church] ever tell the truth!"

Elaine, the divorced shop owner in New York with three children, remembers one nun telling the class that the reason Elaine did not know the answer to a question was because she had gone to public school, and that "those attending public school cannot enter the kingdom of heaven."

One respondent says, "I always felt that I was 'in' with God in a way that my [non-Catholic] friends were not. I also was so zealous that I truly believed, or believed by rote, that no one that thought differently from the Catholic church would be assured of a place in heaven." Another woman "remembers feeling sorry for a good friend of mine because she wasn't Catholic, and so wouldn't be able to go to heaven! *That* was the kind of nonsense I learned in Catholic grade school!"

One of the women remembers wondering, "Is it true that my father, who isn't Catholic, is never going to reach heaven because he doesn't practice the one true faith? . . . Would God really shut him out of eternal happiness just because he's not Catholic? There are a lot of good people who aren't Catholic. Are they going to be shut out, too? I can't believe that. That's wrong. That has to be wrong!"

Another asks, "Did you feel if you had friends who weren't Catholic it was a sin? And never were you to attend service at [a church of] another religion."

Annmarie, the student in New York, notes the church's exclusivity. "One of the times that I was at Mass, I picked up the missalette. In the back of it were the guidelines for receiving communion. It said, 'Only Catholics may receive communion. We hope and pray that all religions can join together in unity. But until then, non-Catholics cannot receive communion.' In other words, until others realize that Catholicism is the best way, other denominations are not welcome to receive communion but are welcome to otherwise participate in the mass. How hypocritical! They divide Catholics . . . [from other] Christians." She adds, "Jesus never said being gay was wrong. He hung out with the outcasts: gays, women, lepers, gentiles. Instead of people reaching to the church for the church's rules and regulations which are blind to reality, blind to humanness, and blind to true spirituality—if they could reach right to Jesus, and say, 'Now what would Jesus want me to do?' [he would probably say] 'The Golden Rule is fundamental.' If you can't . . . follow that, how can you expect to call yourself a Christian, a Catholic?"

Martha articulately describes how her college education changed her way of interpreting scripture, and thus, helped her break away from the church. "My secret guilty skepticism about many of Jesus' miracles was made clean with a sweep of 'Occam's Razor,' a philosophical tenet stating that the simplest explanation is to be preferred over more complex competing theories. Jesus' healing of the possessed boy (Mark 9:14-29) was made no less miraculous by the revelation that the boy was probably epileptic, not possessed by an 'unclean spirit' as the Scripture reads. . . .

"And then there were those loaves and fishes. I learned that the real miracle in Jesus' feeding of the multitudes was that of love. 'Did you think the loaves and fishes just went bloop, bloop?' asked our professor as he pantomimed . . . corn popping. 'Do you think those people would have traveled so far without being adequately prepared?' He went on to describe how Jesus' act of generosity so touched the hearts of the people that they were moved to take out and share the food they had discreetly packed along. The Gospels note that not only was there enough to go around, there were plenty of leftovers.

"For the first time," Martha continues, "the Good News *was* good. It was about the vanquishing of fear. It was about loving. It was *not* about having to accept literal interpretations. As these classroom revelations multiplied, I found my mind and heart flexing with a freedom miraculous in its own right.

"Sin received a different definition, too, as that which alienated a person from self, God, and others.

"And I began to understand how alienated I was from myself, how split I was in my willingness to spout 'acceptable' answers while denying my true beliefs and feelings."

Polly says, "I am saddened by the experience of having grown up Catholic. I am sorry that my early religious education was so narrow—Catholicism did not allow me to feel the joys I now feel in my new religion. . . . I am sorry that I missed many years of the peace that comes with participating in the worship services of a religious community."

Donna tells us "why I won't go back to the Catholic church. . . . They so much look down at and condemn anyone who is divorced, homosexual, had sex without being married, uses birth control. . . . It bothers me very much because I find it to be narrow-minded."

Paula says, "There never seemed to be a 'feeling' in the church I remember going to. It was like a duty."

Another woman compares the Catholic church with others. "The Catholic church is God-focused, whereas other churches are socially oriented or community-oriented. The arrogance that 'we are better' is bullshit."

Geraldine reflects back on years of Catholic training. "Too bad to have learned so much that makes no sense now." She adds, "Catholics . . . for the most part get along by . . . taking from the church what their common sense tells them is usable, and ignoring the rest with a tolerant, nostalgic smile." For many years people did just that. Now, they leave.

On Those Who Stay

What do the women who responded to the survey think of those who are still active in the church?

Glenna thinks that "the Roman Catholic church will survive for some time even with no changes at all. There are always people willing to be dominated, I think, and people willing to ignore the official stand and do as they please." Another agrees: "The only reason that people who are disillusioned with the church stay there is the guilt, or the strongest reason: 'I'll go to hell if I don't go to church every Sunday.' " She is referring to the Catholic Loop; unhappy Catholics are often kept in the loop because they don't want to commit what they have been taught is a sin.

Dottie observes, "What an amazing hierarchical structure and how spellbound the lambs incorporated therein." Kelly adds, "I don't know who's dumber, the nuns or the parishioners for buying the idea that somehow one man is more equal than another."

One of the women notes, "The mass is such that week after week the same words and prayers are spoken over and over again, spoken from memory and out of habit. I can't remember the last time I heard someone say those words and mean it in their hearts." And another "was amazed that I simply dropped out: nobody noticed, nobody cared, nobody said 'Why?' "

Terry sees the same kind of aloofness. "Catholics don't talk in church, even before services. They walk in, they sit down next to someone, and they don't say hello. During mass they shake hands and give the sign of peace. Then they leave without saying goodbye. This can go on week after week for years. I think it is unnatural and unfriendly." And another has noticed that, "Everyone bolts out of church" when mass is over.

Abby says the church is "people attending, not really believing, but it is tradition, it is ethnicity, it is community." Cyndy would agree: "I just . . . read an article in the *New York Times* about being Catholic in America. . . . The article reinforced my own experiences as a Catholic; most Catholics are not really Catholic. They do not *really* believe all that garbage about the body of Christ, the virgin Mary, the infallibility of the pope, and that women are inferior. They tend to focus on the real truths in the Bible—that God is Love, and the greatest commandment is to love your neighbor as yourself, etc., etc. They believe that the church should be there for them, not that they are there for the church. That is what I believe, but I'm not willing to continue to fight those who think that they know better than I do. I cannot change their minds. I don't think that any American will be able to change the minds of the rest of the church."

6

What Is a Church?

By "church," I'm speaking of any religious community, any gathering of like-minded people interested in spirituality. What is a church? What makes a church?

The story that follows attempts to answer these questions.

Danny called at ten o'clock that night with word that our minister, Rev. Lawrence Van Heerden, had died unexpectedly a few hours earlier of a massive coronary.

A fellow church member of mine, Danny tried to keep his voice from choking with grief. " 'Van' was the best. I can't believe it," he managed to say about the vibrant man who had seemed too full of life to ever die, much less at only sixty.

After we talked a few moments, we agreed we should call the other church members. "I'll start by calling Ruth and Rose, and why don't you call Phil and Les," I offered. We then made our calls, and the people we called made their calls, the ripple of shock and grief spreading.

By 11:15 P.M., everyone in our congregation of sixty or so knew. The church network reflected one of our Unitarian Universalist tenets: that we are all part of the interconnecting web of life. A decision was made to hold an informal grief gathering at the church the next evening. We all had to be together to share our disbelief.

Almost everyone came to our gathering. Danny was there, pillar of the church that he is. He's the church's jack-of-all-trades, whose invaluable talents include emergency electrical repairs, plumbing, and an uncanny memory for facts about our one-hundred-year-old building.

Ruth was there, too. A paralegal and member of a military reserve unit, she's also a church board member. She would hold us—and herself—together tonight with her experience in maintaining meeting decorum.

Rose is the part-time church secretary. She first visited our church four years ago when she noticed the people emerging after each service smiling and lingering, reluctant to leave. She came to us then, and she stayed. This day she took time off from her regular job to be at her church desk to answer the dozens of calls that were coming in. She said staying busy all day helped her retain her sanity.

Les, one of our senior members and a former banker, does innumerable tasks around the church without anyone ever knowing about them. His energy puts people half his age to shame. He quietly sat in the back of the sanctuary as people filed in.

Phil, the church's treasurer and perennial cheerleader, could not smile as he hugged everyone, tears streaming down his cheeks.

In came Jeannette, who helps coordinate the church's coffee hour. Though she's seen many deaths in her years, she said, "This is a bad one, a tough one."

Carolyn, Linda, Margaret, Len, Jeff, Joe, Jim, Scott, Hope, Claudette, and Don were at the gathering. So were Jim and Lucille, new members originally from the Midwest; along with Ed, another new member; and Laura, a richly talented pianist and a church member for most of her life. Longtime members Fred and Bertha were in the pews, as were Debbie and Kareene, and Bonnie, whose marks are everywhere you look in the church, especially in the Sunday school. Bob and Lillian, as always, played the organ. Denise and Bob, railroad enthusiasts, stood in the back, holding each other. Dot, our poet, dabbed at her eyes.

Some area Unitarian Universalist ministers also joined us as we sang a few hymns. We wept through a duet, one of Van's favorite songs, sung by Lisa and Suzannah. No one knew where they got the strength to be so composed. Then we each stood and made personal testimonials about Van, recounting his lessons to us. And we could all still see his smile and hear his laugh, our favorite memories of him.

We cried, we hugged, we murmured reassurances, we mourned our loss. How could we go on? Van was perfect for our small church. This was so unfair!

Van was an oratorical genius. His sermons not only held meaning for each member of this diverse little congregation—whether Christian, atheist, New Age, or agnostic—but they also often moved us to tears, made us angry at injustice, *and* made us laugh.

He was a feminist, and a counselor sought out by men who wanted his advice and guidance because he'd had his share of life's pain, yet he'd also had his joys that pulled him through.

He loved the children, and they loved him. A child's dedication, called a baptism in other religions, when officiated by Van was reason alone to come to a service.

He advised the various committees, injecting humor when proceedings were getting too serious.

He was an avid movie buff, often lacing his sermons with descriptions of scenes from something he saw a few nights earlier.

He fairly sparkled with the joy of living.

Without him to guide us, how could the church continue to grow? How could we keep moving forward? Many of us had such thoughts that night.

I looked through my tears at the faces of our members— Ruth, Rose, Dan, Les, Phil, and all the others. Men were unabashedly weeping. Women were hugging. Hands were touching, holding, comforting.

Then I realized: *This* is what makes a church. It's not the relics or the steeple or the sanctuary. It's not the candles or the flowers or even the dogma. Yes, all these things are important; they emphasize purpose or add focus and grace.

And it's not the minister. Oh yes, ministers have a major influence. They serve as a rudder.

But it's the *people* of a church who work the ship and determine the direction. In the end, it's the people, the members, who are a church, a community of believers who come together to share— to join in prayer, to donate their talents, to share what they have in common, and to recognize the beauty of their differences, all of this in joy and sometimes in grief. They're family, certainly, and even better, a loving family they each have *chosen*.

That is why our little church will go on without Van and will probably last another one hundred years. We'll miss Van; we're bound to make a few avoidable mistakes without him. But we'll always thank Van for showing us how terrific we are. That was his gift to us. Our gift to him was to help make his light shine ever brighter.

But our gift to each other, and to the community around us, is to spread those ripples of sharing, our community of prayer and joy, and yes, at times even grief, beyond our church walls. *That's* what a church is. It's the spirit of many people. And one death, however much it hurts, can't take that spirit away.

I wrote and published the above in 1991 when my church's minister died unexpectedly. His death really brought home the reality that a church *is* the people who belong to it and keep it going.

In the preface to this book, I make reference to the feeling I had when visiting two different Catholic churches for mass, after my father died. I likened it to a train platform full of waiting people, angry they have been kept waiting yet powerless to change their situation.

Yet when that anger is expressed, especially by women, some see it as useless complaining. Are the women interviewed and surveyed here "just a bunch of whiners who should just get on with their lives"?

What would the women say in response to this kind of comment?

Martha says, "I did get on with my life. I finally came to the realization that I was getting nowhere trying to make myself heard in any fashion by anyone in authority in the Roman Catholic church. There simply isn't any legitimate forum in this church for expressing complaints or differences. When I found myself 'spinning my wheels' and generating bitterness instead of progress, I knew it was time to invest my energies elsewhere. That is when I left Roman Catholicism." Martha is now an Episcopalian.

"I *am* 'getting on with my life,'" says Cyndy. "That's why I am a member of the Unitarian Universalist church and a successful executive. Recognizing the damage done to my psyche by the subtle teachings of the Catholic church was the first step in my healing process. I am not whining—I am trying to communicate the problem so that others can recognize it and prevent other women from viewing themselves as worthless or their feelings as wrong."

"My life never stopped," adds Margo, now a Congregationalist. "Whining is for infants. When I realized the Catholic church was not for me I took a different road and 'that has made all the difference.' "

Chris believes, "It's hard, I'm sure, for a person who's not been raised Catholic to understand the impact of being raised in the 'faith.' In fact, it's difficult for those who *have* experienced it to fathom what it's done [to people]! . . . The women in this book are trying very hard to get on with their lives! . . .

"By discussing our lives and experiences, we are practicing to live new lives, free of our pasts. Incidentally, while some of us try to move on, the Catholic influence still exists. . . . There are a lot of continuing influences and strings pulling on women raised Catholic—they aren't easy to overcome. You're born Catholic, and it sometimes feels like that label is tattooed on your face, even if you've decided to leave the religion."

"Verbalizing all this *is* getting on with our lives," Hillary maintains. "Part of getting on with our lives is discovering that other women share the same experiences and feelings growing up Catholic. In the 1960s, as we left parochial schools and ultimately the church, it was like coming out of the dark ages and recovering from the scare tactics used by priests and nuns. We were brainwashed—the only people I met with the same rigid ideas, unrealistic fears, and lost spontaneity were Catholic girls."

Calling the women "whiners," according to Abby, is "a silly criticism. Being able to call something for what it is is not whining. . . . It is important that people call it the way they see it. That hasn't prevented me from going on with my life. Actually, it's quite the contrary: I feel the kinds of criticisms I have about the Catholic church have actually been motivators to keep me on my journey and to keep me going on with my life and finding other ways to . . . express my spirituality."

Donna guesses that "it is probably a male saying this. . . . To this person I would say, 'You are obviously blind. These women are stating facts about their upbringing and how they were treated. Most, if not all, have left the church. This book was written to bring it out in the open.' . . . This person is also insecure and maybe a little worried about how women are standing up and hopefully making change occur."

Maggie's retort to this question is, "I guess one could say the Jewish survivors of the Holocaust should do that [just get on with their lives] also! Or the blacks! Or the American Indians! People do terrible things and then they want their victims to just rise above it."

Does Anyone Even Listen to the Bishops Anymore?

Q. 146: Did Christ intend that this power [to teach, to sanctify, and to rule the members of His church] should be exercised by the apostles alone?

Answer: No, Christ intended that this power should be exercised also by their successors, the bishops of the church.

Q. 149: Who assist the bishops in the care of souls?

Answer: The priests, especially parish priests, assist the bishops in the care of souls.
—*The New Baltimore Catechism* (pp. 66-67)

What makes a church? The Roman Catholic church hierarchy seems to believe "the church" is the men running it. When the women were asked about this, and in particular about a U.S. bishops' pronouncement in late 1993 that husbands should help their wives with household tasks and child-rearing, the reactions of the women ranged from outright laughter to disgust.

"What planet have they been on?" asks Hillary, the designer and mother of two from Connecticut.

Chris adds, "If I felt this was going to be the beginning of more widespread reform, I'd cheer. Unfortunately, I think this is a lame attempt at pacifying the Catholic population. It's a microscopic concession to the need for reform. In many cases, the pronouncement means nothing since many men already help with such tasks. It reflects how backward and out of touch the church is!"

Abby asks, "Why would it be men 'helping' women with housework and child-rearing? . . . The whole emphasis on 'helping' women with these tasks . . . fits in with the bishops' idea of [seeing] men and women in this big gender separation which they [the bishops] continue to encourage in their flocks. It's silly, and it points out how misogynist they really are. . . . It's too bad that the bishops don't see that the stronger marriages and better marriages are partnerships, and this kind of rigid gender-sorting of tasks just creates more anger . . . in relationships. This kind of comment really grates on me. . . .

"The other thing is that whenever I hear of U.S. bishops' pronouncements, I guess I wonder, 'Who cares?' The Catholic women I am in contact with . . . are feminist . . . and try to somehow make sense out of Catholicism by taking what they feel are Jesus' messages and making *those* part of their life and not buying into the bureaucratic end of Catholicism. Thinking women in the church who I know don't really care what the bishops have to say."

Maggie makes a point: "Too little, too late! Besides, what gave them the idea that the men who don't help, *would* because the bishops said they should? They [the bishops] seem to have an exaggerated sense of their own importance. The men who do 'help' around the house do so because they care about their families."

Kathleen says, "Well, bishops, welcome to the twentieth century! . . . I guess . . . I could say that the value of the wife and mother has finally been validated, but why now? Hasn't this work always been valuable?"

Donna suspects that the bishops are making such pronouncements due to "financial pressure," and Phyllis asks, "I wonder who's doing the bishops' household tasks?"

Others take this news more at face value. "I am pleased for the old-fashioned thinkers who will abide by the pronouncements and make the women's tasks lighter. How odd that a bishop dictates equality between the sexes. How 1800s." So says Margo. Agreeing with her is Cyndy, who adds, "Roles within a marriage should be defined by the wants, skills, and desires of the people involved—not defined by sex." One can sense the skeptical attitude these women have.

Martha states her hopes most eloquently: "I applaud the bishops' efforts to encourage men to help women with household tasks and child-rearing. It's one step in the right direction, one objective along the road to the larger goal of bestowing upon women the same respect and dignity that men have been accorded by the church all along. Perhaps, someday, a new generation of bishops will encourage women to help men at the altar and in the confessional. Then men and women could share vestments as well as aprons."

7

So Far Ahead That We're Behind

Appendix Question IV: How can we prove that all men are obliged to practice religion?

Answer: We can prove that all men are obliged to practice religion because all men are entirely dependent on God, and must recognize that dependence by honoring Him and praying to Him.

— *The New Baltimore Catechism* (p. 216)

One cannot examine ex-Catholic (or even still-Catholic, or any other faith, for that matter) women's spirituality today, or our roles in worship, without being aware of the massive amount of research and study that has taken place in the last five to ten years. Certainly there are earlier writings about matriarchy, women, God, and religion, but until the mid-1980s, one could go into a bookstore or library and find only a handful, literally, of books on these subjects. Today we can see whole sections of books, from floor to ceiling, on women and religion.

The voices you hear in the other ten chapters of this book are of women I've called "ordinary," a term I use with awe because what I mean is "powerful because they are so real, so part of everyday life." But I could not neglect the women who have studied women and religion. These are the women whose books now fill the new shelves in the stores and libraries. Their voices have made a major difference in our thinking, the thinking of women *and* men about who we are on this planet. So I added their wise words here to help explain how women got into this patriarchal "trap," as one of them calls it; their words also corroborate what the ex-Catholic women say throughout this book.

From Matriarchy to Patriarchy to What?

Scholar Elizabeth Dodson Gray defines "patriarchy" as "a culture that is slanted so that men are valued a lot and women are valued less; . . . in which men's prestige is up, women's prestige is down." Matriarchy would be defined in the reverse. Dodson Gray says neither is preferable, that a balanced blend is the ideal (Dodson Gray, p. 19).

Historian Gerda Lerner's work traces goddess religions through to patriarchy. She discusses how it happened, but at the same time, she also seems to implicitly answer the question that titles the previous chapter: What is a church? Her answer: the people, because they make their religion serve *them.*

As Lerner tells it, there were many goddesses worshipped by people in the ancient world, 3,000 years before Christ's birth. She says, "Mental constructs cannot be created from a void; they always reflect events and concepts of historic human beings in society." She goes on to say, "While we cannot say with certainty that certain political and economic changes 'caused' changes in religious beliefs and myths, we cannot help but notice a pattern in the changes of religious beliefs in a number of societies, following upon or concurrent with certain societal changes" (Lerner, pp. 144–45). Today, evidence of this is that the awareness of changes in women's (and men's) roles is causing churches to change their liturgies to use more inclusive language, e.g., "He or She."

In those days, however, the Great Goddess, as she was known, represented all of creation: the earth and the universe, humans as well as animals and nature, and life and death. "The duality of the Goddess represented the duality observable in nature— night and day, birth and death, light and darkness. Thus, in the earlier known phases of religious worship the female force was recognized as awesome, powerful, transcendent," says Lerner. New life, birth, fertility, and sexuality were all worshipped in honor of the Great Goddess (Lerner, pp. 148–49).

Lerner says that as people grew to know more how humans reproduced, and as we moved from being a nomadic species to one practicing agriculture, the male began to take on a stronger role as a partner to the Great Goddess. And as warfare became a more organized venture, kings became a more dominant force in society (Lerner, p. 152).

Over time, the Great Goddess "not only loses her supremacy but generally becomes domesticated and transformed into the supreme god's wife," reflecting the emergence of male-dominated monarchies, with the king more powerful than the queen. The Great Goddess begins to no longer represent all of life, but now her power is split and given over to more minor goddesses— one for fertility, one for birth, another for sexuality, and so forth (Lerner, p. 159). In our time, do we see the women saints as goddesses of a sort, protecting other attributes than the ancient ones the goddesses protected?

Parallel to these developments, humanity began to trace a person's lineage less and less through the mother's line and more and more through the father's (Lerner, p. 154). Tracing one's heritage this way, kings could designate their successor. (Later, this would become an important way of controlling women's behavior.) And then, some goddesses' names were changed from female to male. "King" and "father" came to be the names of one of the male gods (Lerner, p. 157).

Merlin Stone's *When God Was a Woman* describes how men insisting on tracing one's lineage through the males in the family ("patrilineal") established further control over women. "Inherent within the very practice of sexual customs [in the Near and Middle East] was the lack of concern for the *paternity* of children— and it is only with a certain knowledge of paternity that a patrilineal system can be maintained. . . . These ancient sexual customs were finally denounced as wicked and depraved and that it was for this reason that the Levite priests devised the concept of sexual 'morality': premarital virginity for *women*, marital fidelity for *women*, in other words total control over the knowledge of paternity" (Stone, p. 161). Women under the goddess system who had been considered holy were seen by the god system as impure, immoral. Who can't remember the Charlton Heston Bible movies, with Moses as hero, riding in on his chariot to clear the temple of the "prostitutes"?

Scholar Elaine Pagels, in *The Gnostic Gospels,* maintains that Peter was threatened by women, because Christ first revealed himself to a woman, Mary Magdelene, when he arose from the dead, and second, because Christ often included Magdelene in with the male apostles. At times Christ seemed to favor her, which provoked jealousy in Peter. Another apostle, Levi, scolded Peter at one point, saying, "Peter, you have always been hot-tempered. . . . If the Savior made her worthy, who are you to reject her?" (Pagels, p. 15).

Was it Peter who devalued her by calling her a prostitute? Through the ages Mary Magdelene became this symbol of the worst kind of person, having committed the worst kind of sins, the bottom of the bottom. But she still proved useful to Peter: she became representative of how awful a person could be yet *even she* was someone Christ could forgive. How generous Peter was!

Paul picked up on these themes and incorporated them into his writings; indeed, anyone who has listened to those who proselytize door-to-door has heard his "women be silent" quote.

In *Eunuchs for the Kingdom of Heaven*, Uta Ranke-Heinemann maintains that, "At the root of the defamation of women in the Church lies the notion that women are unclean and, as such, stand in opposition to the holy." She quotes Clement, the bishop of Alexandria, who wrote, "With women 'the very consciousness of their own nature must evoke feelings of shame' " (Ranke-Heinemann, p. 127).

Augustine (354–430) "took the contempt for sex that saturates the work of the Church Fathers, . . . and to it he added a new factor: A personal and theological sexual anxiety" (Ranke-Heinemann, p. 76).

It was Augustine who tied original sin to the pleasure of sex. "Augustine thought that when Adam and Eve disobeyed God and ate the forbidden fruit of Paradise, 'they were ashamed and covered their sexual parts with fig leaves.' He concludes from this that 'this is where it comes from.' . . . He means that what they were both trying to hide was the place whence the first sin is transmitted. . . . Thus, according to Augustine, sexual intercourse, or more precisely, sexual pleasure is what carries original sin on and on, from generation to generation" (p. 77). Ranke-Heinemann adds that Augustine maintained that since Christ was "conceived without any fleshly pleasure," he had no original sin (p. 78). This concept instilled the belief in places like limbo, a place for unbaptized innocents, and much anxiety—

some of it described by the women, in chapter 5—over having their unbaptized babies die. Ranke-Heinemann makes a tongue-in-cheek conclusion: "God himself has pronounced the child guilty, evidently because of an offense so bad that to punish it he wishes not to associate with this child for all eternity, which means, for the child, eternal death. In order to snatch the child from God's hangman's hands and to lay it instead in God's loving hands, one must simply baptize the child" (pp. 309–10).

Ranke-Heinemann notes that before his conversion, Augustine was a Manichaean, a sect whose beliefs included enjoyment of sexual pleasure, but with contraception, because they felt the earth belonged to the devil, so why populate it. After his conversion, Augustine's "affirmation of pleasure and denial of procreation . . . turned into an affirmation of procreation and a denial of pleasure" (p. 80). Augustine also put a high value on virginity, because it avoids lust (p. 97).

Tie this in with Augustine's only justification for marriage and sex—that of having children—and it explains how the Catholic church has been so anti-contraception over the ages.

The book of Genesis tells us that because of Eve, women will have pain in childbirth. Augustine concluded, then, that Mary "conceived Jesus virginally, without having to be ashamed about lust, and for that reason she also gave birth painlessly" (p. 93). Many women here were taught these beliefs in the mid- and latter-twentieth century.

Ranke-Heinemann tells a chilling story that illustrates men's belief that women *should* experience pain in childbirth due to Eve's sin. "In 1853 English theologians brought charges against Queen Victoria's personal physician, reproaching him for anesthetizing the queen during childbirth" (p. 296).

Prior to converting, Augustine betrayed a former lover by seeing another woman. "Augustine's pessimistic sexual morality is simply a repression of his bad sexual conscience, his aversion to women a continual ferreting out of the culpable cause of his failure," says Ranke-Heinemann (p. 80).

Thomas Aquinas (1225–1274) wasn't much of an improvement. He said, "I don't see what sort of help woman was created to provide man with, if one excludes the purpose of procreation. If woman is not given to man for help in bearing children, for what help could she be? To till the earth together?" (p. 88). It was Aquinas who defined woman's roles as being primarily with children, in the kitchen and home, and helping in the church, which Ranke-Heinemann says is "an idea that still has life in it, in fact it continues to be the Catholic hierarchy's primary theological position on woman" (p. 88).

The church's focus on sex and contraception is crucial in defining its view of women, and it encapsulates its fears about Catholics using birth control. And with birth control comes fewer people for the church, less money for its coffers, and less stability for its power and future. Ranke-Heinemann quotes a 1977 German Catholic clergy journal that editorialized, "It is quite certain that in the next ten to twenty years, the 'pill' will crush the growth of the Church, with all the consequences this will have for the next generation of priests and religious, as well as for the yield on church taxes. No more new church buildings will be needed. . . . What will happen precisely . . . why people were warned against the propaganda for the 'pill,' namely: an alarming drop in the birth rate, a demoralization of society. . . . Public contempt for chastity, resulting in a decline of the social prestige of priests and religious" (p. 297).

This forecast was correct, if one has viewed the merging of parishes and closing of Catholic schools, and the decline in seminary students, over the last twenty-five years or so.

Many church fathers since Aquinas have continued with his

and Augustine's thinking about women through the teachings on sex and birth control. Pope Paul VI in 1968 condemned contraceptives. One reason he did so was because, "Men who have become accustomed to using contraceptives could lose their respect for woman," a stand Ranke-Heinemann says projects "their lack of respect for women to husbands" (p. 296).

Pope John Paul II, in 1984, cautioned couples to use the rhythm method correctly and not "for dishonest reasons to keep [the number of children] below the birthrate that is morally right for their family" (p. 84). Perhaps even more of a stretch, in 1987 John Paul II affirmed that Mary's hymen was never broken (p. 347). It seems embarrassing for a man whose regard for women is so questionable, to have such a detailed biological discussion about women; it's like Strom Thurmond discussing whether or not human life begins at conception—they know not of what they speak.

The advent of RU 486, the so-called "abortion pill," has enraged the church hierarchy as well as extreme anti-abortion groups. Their anger is disguised by their concern for the fetus. One cannot help but think the pill really symbolizes power that these parties do not want women to have.

And lest one thinks that times have changed, 1994 saw the public transit authority in heavily Catholic Boston attempt to ban explicit public service ads on trains and buses for condom use for the prevention of AIDS. Imagine the furor if the ads were promoting contraception!

While the men of the church have not wanted to change, women still within the Catholic church have been making their own changes. These women are attempting to recreate it in various ways. In *Women-Church: Theology and Practice*, Dr. Rosemary Radford Ruether describes new liturgies that address women's needs, needs that the traditional church ignores. For example, there is within Women-Church a rite of healing after rape. The women participating verbally and nonverbally validate the violence of the rape, then go on to tell the woman she is still someone with integrity and beauty. The rite ends with prayers to the Mother-Spirit of Original Blessing for the woman's healing (Radford Reuther, pp. 158–59). A similar ceremony takes place for a home in which violence or burglary has taken place; its purpose is to eradicate the feelings of invasion and powerlessness so that one can live there peacefully again. And another rite addresses the grief that often accompanies miscarriage (pp. 162–63).

Radford Reuther says, "The key to the erasure of women in religious history, as in all of patriarchal history, is not that women were inactive, but that they have not been able to shape the tradition by which the story of what they have done is remembered and carried on" (p. 43). These new liturgies are a way to correct this omission.

Women-Church gatherings are not mock masses; in fact, they are deliberately different and deliberately smaller. One woman, still a Catholic, who participates in a monthly Women-Church group, described a meeting to me. "It's certainly not what the pope would consider 'Catholic'!" she said. "We call the twelve of us 'Great Women.' We do have bread and wine but we do not imitate a mass. The goal here is to have these small religious gatherings in many homes or places within a community, not to have a cathedral run by women.

"Our end-of-the-year gathering focused on the theme of 'saying goodbye.' We could say goodbye to anything that we wanted to get rid of, so we could start the new year fresh and renewed. We took colored paper, and cut it into fall leaf shapes. On each leaf, we wrote down something we wanted to get rid of—perhaps an old grudge, or pain from a failed relationship.

"Then we tied each leaf to an inflated balloon. We walked

to an open area in a nearby park, stood in a circle, and talked about what each of us was letting go. We sang a hymn, then said a prayer, then let go of our balloons with the leaves. As they began to float away, we found ourselves screaming and yelling with joy, hugging and laughing and crying. It was spontaneous, and wonderful."

Very different than "the sacrifice of the mass," isn't it! But one can hear how deeply it touched the lives of those women. Mary Jo Weaver, in *Springs of Water in a Dry Land*, says that the men of the traditional church view such women as "renegades, heretics, or in some other way effectively 'out of the church.' " She explains, "The attempt on the part of Catholic women to redefine themselves as church, while it may be a metaphorical flight to the wilderness, is not a rejection of [Roman Catholic] . . . tradition. Rather than leaving the church, those involved in the Womenchurch movement are abandoning a model of church life that is no longer persuasive" (p. 63).

Carol Ochs, in *Behind the Sex of God*, declares "that a matriarchal or patriarchal religion is more than a religion in which the central deity is female or male. It involves our relationship to other beings, how we confront death, how we find meaning, and other important concerns. In short, the matriarchal or patriarchal character of our religion determines how we order our values. Matriarchy and patriarchy are two fundamental and opposing ways of life in this world and of understanding reality" (p. 110). Ochs gives us reasons to understand why this issue is vital today to many people exploring new ways of worship.

Even some men within the church are rejecting the traditional ways. Called the "Father of Liberation Theology," which encourages the underclass to fight for their economic and political rights, Leonardo Boff of Brazil says, "I resigned from the official church, with priests and parishes, but not from the popular church. When the people ask, I celebrate [mass]. . . . Jesus was a layman. The biggest disgrace of a bishop or a pope is that he forgets he's one of the people. He thinks he was born a boss. . . . I promoted myself to layman. . . . Until the 1980s, I was confident the church could be reformed and become more open to women, laymen, and the poor. I don't believe that anymore. This type of clerical, authoritarian, sexist, centralizing Church has no salvation." For his outspokenness, Father Boff has been penalized by Rome, which accepts no renegades, even male ones. "There's a religious marketplace out there. And the Catholic church is losing out because it offers a very bad product: doctrinaire and formal." Father Boff's mass, according to this article, "is more like a block party. . . . [A]t other times, mass takes on the trappings and music of Brazil's popular African-based spirit religions." Boff's communities are growing, and are now counted at approximately seven million Catholic members. This worries the church in Brazil, because about 900,000 people a year leave the traditional church there (*Patriot Ledger*, December 31, 1993).

Does the emergence of these new forms of worship, Women-Church, and New Age and other return-to-the-Goddess movements mean we are headed back (or ahead) to matriarchy? For those women who have replaced "God" with "Goddess," that is apparently true. Weaver says, "Patriarchal Catholicism [and other male-dominated religions, I would add] worships a limited God and demands that women fit into a spiritual system where we cannot, by definition, find a place for ourselves. . . . I believe that many women in the church are homeless because we attempt to worship a Being whose attributes do not resonate with our experience. We suffer because we try to fit our spiritual aspirations into a space that is more restrictive and less magnificent than we know to be true" (p. 11). Many women have said, "I left the Catholic church to find that magnificence somewhere else."

Sometime ago there was a cartoon in the newspaper about alternative energy sources and energy companies. In several panels, the energy company executive says pompously, "You want oil for energy? We can get you oil." "You want natural gas for energy? We can get you natural gas." "You want water power for energy? We'll get you water power." But he looks worried in the last panel when he says, "You want solar power for energy? Uh—solar power isn't feasible!"

Just like the energy company cannot own the sun like they own the oil wells and dams, the church fathers cannot somehow profit by women forming their own liturgies and making their own way. So they discredit the women. Elizabeth Dodson Gray talks about Carol Christ, the Yale theologian, who studied the spiritual connection between women and nature. "Nearly every male theologian . . . told her, 'That's not religion—nature worship perhaps, but not religion.' What we now know they were saying was, 'That is not religion as we male theologians have developed it.' " Dodson Gray goes on to say "that women have a very interesting and different religious consciousness which includes a strong sense of connectedness to the natural world" (pp. 124–25). Perhaps this explains the appeal to many women of New Age, earth-oriented philosophies. Many men are attracted to this nature-oriented thinking as well. Perhaps, also, returning to forms of goddess- and nature-worship puts us "so far behind" (back to our roots) that we're really *ahead* of the patriarchy.

Matriarchy to patriarchy to something new? Perhaps that is what these writers are describing. They, and the women who have left the Roman Catholic church, are really asking us to think about this question: Suppose the way we view the Judeo-Christian God is not "given" to us by God, but is, instead, an idea foisted upon society for the last two thousand years by certain men with their own, very human agenda? This question asks us to challenge just about every notion we as Westerners have about our deity.

At various points in human history, we have changed our view of the nature of God. Perhaps today women—because so many women are dissatisfied with the old, male-only version—are fostering as profound a change in our thinking. We are living in exhilarating times.

8

Exploration

Q.206: Why does a Catholic sin against faith by taking part in non-Catholic worship?

Answer: A Catholic sins against faith by taking part in non-Catholic worship because he thus professes belief in a religion he knows is false.

—*The New Baltimore Catechism* (p. 96)

A Catholic colleague of mine once marveled to me how much she admired non-Catholics because, "You people go to church even though you don't have to!"

After a lifetime of being taught that Catholicism is the only true faith, and of seeing the huge numbers of Catholics going to mass alongside them, many Catholics are surprised to see many other churches thrive. Fear, taught through such methods as the catechism words above, has short-circuited anything more than a mild curiosity by Catholics in other religions. And, somehow, the ex-Catholic, who may have long ago disengaged herself from the church of her upbringing, still carries that fear with her.

How do you find a new religion? a new church? There isn't much in religious literature about "shopping" for a new church, possibly because virtually all denominations do not wish to appear predatory for members of other denominations. Instead, they aim their appeals at the "unchurched."

Church and synagogue advertising is usually subtle. A church may call itself "the friendly church" or one where you will find "healing and love." Their advertisements appear in the Saturday edition of most daily newspapers, with the times of their services and church school.

My experience has been that when people are looking for a new church, they look for a new church *and* a new religion at the same time, and they look first not at these advertisements but instead they thumb through—of all things—the Yellow Pages. They start with those listed, and they visit the ones that sound interesting to them. As much as you might think people would follow some more elegant process, in reality, it's not unlike looking for a car.

When I was searching for a church, I put a lot of stock in what the churches "stood for," perhaps more than most people would. I asked people I respected about denominations: what were their practices? what did they believe? what were their "rules and regulations" for members? what were their services like? More than one person pointed me in the same direction— Unitarian Universalism—and because I had known members of that denomination from political work fifteen years before, I was open to further exploration.

Most people, however—and you would probably be among them—first want to know the "feel" of a church. Yes, they pay attention to the stated beliefs and practices of that church, but their ultimate decision is based on how they connect with those in the congregation *and* how they connect with the worshipping that takes place.

Once I narrowed my choice down to the one denomination,

I then visited local churches of that faith. In one, I felt a connection both with the people at the service, and with the service itself; however, the minister made it clear he was to be the center of attention during the service, and that was a turn-off for me. So I visited another, where the minister counted himself as among the worshippers, not the leader of them. After several visits, that was the church I joined.

I'm not suggesting you treat church visits as if you were kicking car tires. It's far more personal and complex a process than that. But without attending a regular service—don't just talk with the minister or rabbi or church member, but attend a real, regular service—you can't get to know a denomination or congregation. At one of the first services I ever attended at a Unitarian Universalist church, there was a post-service churchwide meeting about a piece of real estate that church owned, and what could be done with it. I stayed in my pew and listened.

During that rather mundane meeting I learned several important things I hadn't realized I wanted to know: I saw that the members owned and ran their church. I saw that the minister did not dictate policy to the members but instead served as an advisor. I felt the cohesion of their gathering around common goals and objectives that had evolved over time. And I learned there was a wisdom that even the most unsophisticated person there had, about how central their church was to their lives. Despite the members' embarrassed apologies during the coffee hour later on that they'd had this meeting on the same Sunday I happened to visit, this was the church I eventually joined. I had seen all I needed to see to tell me I could be happy here. Almost ten years later, I am still a member.

So visit the house of worship during a regular service. Pay attention to your feelings about the gathering. You may find yourself comparing the church to what you remember about the last Catholic church you attended. As I say in the introduction to this book, the difference in symbols was the first comparison I made. Perhaps just crossing the threshold to a new church is the only push you need to explore further. Or it may just turn you off because it will seem alien: you may not be able to forget holy water, vestments, stations of the cross, the crucifix, statues, and you may find yourself looking for them in some unconscious way just to see something familiar. Keep in mind that you will not find most other churches to be similar in appearance to the Catholic church. How you react to this will tell you if you will feel comfortable in a non-Catholic church.

Some congregations may not even have a house of worship. They may be too small to afford one, and may instead meet as a fellowship in a meeting room or hall. Many Quaker groups meet this way. Others rent the sanctuary of another church, even of another denomination. These meetings underscore that "a church" is not a building but is really the community of people coming together. If you are open to this kind of worship experience, you may find a small church with which you will be happy.

One of the first things I felt is something I hope you feel: a profound thanks that the founders of this wonderful country had the wisdom to secure us freedom of religion, and separation of church and state. In your search, you will relish these.

But first, read through this checklist about yourself. It will tell you in which direction to head.

A Religion Checklist

Answer the following questions about yourself and your beliefs. Write down the answers. You may want to do this over a period of time, and not all in one sitting, because you will probably have more thoughts to add.

- How do I imagine God?

- What are rituals and symbols that I'd like?

- Is music important to me as part of worship?

- What are the "myths" (stories) I believe in—Adam and Eve, Noah's Ark, etc.?

- Do I pray? If so, what form does it take? Who/what am I praying to?

- What moves me, what strikes me with awe?

- What kinds of guides to behavior do I want to have for me and my children?

- What kind of religious education do I want for my children? And how do I want it taught to them?

- What is a doctrine I could believe in? What would repulse me?

When visiting a church/house of worship, be able to answer these questions:

- What is the church's doctrine, what is their theology, what do they stand for/against on the issues of the day?

- What rituals and symbols did I like/not like?

- What roles do women, men, and children play in the church's ongoing life? And how do they interact with each other, and with the minister/clergyperson? Can women be clergy?

- What are the church's "myths"—in other words, what are the stories believed to be true by the members, and what do I think of these stories?

- How did the people approach me? Did they make me feel welcome? What do they say about their church, their religion? What about the clergy—how did I feel meeting them?

You might want to discuss the answers with your spouse/partner, children, or friends, to help you sort out your thoughts and feelings.

Snapshots of Many Choices

What follows is a list of religious denominations in the United States. You can see if they match what you've written down in your answers to the religion checklist.

There are wonderful guidebooks that can define each religion that you'll find in the United States. To gather information for this chapter, I have drawn on three of these: J. Gordon Melton, *The Encyclopedia of American Religions* (Detroit: Gale Research, 1989); Peter Bishop and Michael Darton (eds.), *The Encyclopedia of World Faiths* (New York: Facts on File Publications, 1988); and Benson Y. Landis, *World Religions* (New York: Dutton, 1965).

The summary, which follows, lists several of the more well-known religious denominations found in the United States. Your search may be wider, and may include visits to lesser-known, smaller groups.

Adventists/Seventh-day. Members believe in the physical return of Jesus Christ, called the second advent. In the first days of this church (early 1800s), specific dates for the return of Jesus were forecast; some sects still choose dates. They believe in the Trinity of the Eternal Father, Son of the Eternal Father, and the Holy Spirit. Jesus, the son of God, became human, died for human sins, rose from the dead, and is in heaven petitioning the Father and Holy Spirit for us. Baptism is by immersion. Believers do not use intoxicating drinks, tobacco, or narcotics. Many are vegetarians. Tithes (one-tenth of one's income) and offerings support the church. Attention is to signs that foretell the second coming of Christ. Sunday services are informal, and feature hymns, reading of Scripture, prayers, a sermon, and offering. Individual churches are self-governing but take guidance from the conference of which it is a member. Adventists have a large foreign mission, and the denomination has built many hospitals.

Baptists. Baptists are grouped as American Baptists or as Southern Baptists. They believe in the New Testament. They were founded in the United States in 1639 by Roger Williams (1603?– 1683). Baptism is by immersion. There is no official statement of creed, because that would imply human authority in the church. Southern Baptist churches (usually in the southern and western United States) and Northern (now called American) Baptist churches each went their own way when they disagreed over slavery, and then evolution. There are two sacraments: baptism and the Lord's supper. They draw validity and inspiration from the Scriptures, believe in the immortality of the soul, the need of redemption from sin, and in the brotherhood of man. Services take no one form or order of worship, but are determined by the local congregation; usually hymns, prayers, a sermon, Scripture reading, and an offering take place. Local churches control their own activities but the convention that the church belongs to guides it. Today the Southern Baptist convention is fundamentalist, believing God himself wrote the Bible, so they take it literally, while the American Baptist convention is considered more liberal on current social issues.

Christian Science/Church of Christ, Scientist. This denomination was founded by a woman, Mary Baker Eddy (1821–1910), in the 1870s. Members believe the teachings in the Bible can be interpreted as a science that can heal the body (and any human need) by mental or spiritual regeneration. Mary Baker Eddy's beliefs grew from her own healing of an injury when she was reading Matthew. She believed that God caused and healed disease. It was her premise that Christianity always held the potential to heal but that over the centuries that power was lost, and she wanted a church that would bring back those beliefs. Christian Scientists believe Jesus is the Savior of Humanity. Services are Sundays, and the focus is on a lesson-sermon, composed of readings from Mrs. Eddy's book, *Science and Health, With Key to the Scriptures,* and from the Bible. On Wednesday evenings, there are testimony meetings. Visitors can go to Reading Rooms, where there are Mary Baker Eddy materials they can read.

Congregational/United Church of Christ. Depending on where you are in the country, either of these names would be given to one of these churches. The denomination was formed in 1957 upon the merger of the Congregational Christian, Evangelical Protestant, and Reformed churches. The church has its roots in England, from where its adherents had to flee in the 1600s; the Pilgrims of Plymouth were of this denomination, then known as Puritans. Each local church can formulate its own statement of doctrines, with some following a basic "platform" adopted by the church's leadership council. Each member has a voice in church decisions. Most Sunday services are composed of hymns, scripture readings, prayer, a sermon, and an offering. UCC members believe in the Trinity and in baptism. The denomination is considered socially liberal and is active in peace and justice issues.

Eastern Orthodox. Also known as "Greek Catholic," members do not recognize the primacy of the pope, the belief in Mary's immaculate conception, nor in the use of carved images. They do revere relics of saints, pictures of holy objects, and the cross. Confession is less common than in the Roman church, and daily mass is not essential. Priests may be married before they are ordained.

Episcopal. This was first known as the Church of England or Anglican church when its first U.S. church was founded in Jamestown in 1609. The "high" church members follow many Roman traditions, especially in ceremonies; many ex-Catholics are comfortable with this church because so much of what they experience is familiar. The "low" church is opposed to ceremony, and the focus is instead on reading and preaching Christ's word. The denomination uses the Book of Common Prayer, written in the 1920s. Those called Episcopalian are considered liberal, pro-human rights and justice, and ordain women. The Anglicans are more conservative, and oppose the ordination of women; this issue is currently quite divisive for the denomination.

Friends (Religious Society of Friends or Quakers). This group was founded in the 1600s in England by people who thought that Christian churches at the time were ignoring the spiritual aspects of Christianity. They emphasized "the inner light," and called themselves Friends of Truth, then became the Religious Society of Friends. Observers thought they "quaked" at the word of God, thus the nickname. There is no formal creed. They emphasize feeling the Holy Spirit, "the Light Within." They teach peace and nonresistance. There are no clergy at most meetings. Services are very informal, with anyone able to speak when they are so moved.

Jehovah's Witnesses. Founded in Pennsylvania in the 1870s, Witnesses believe that the Bible says Jesus will begin a new world after destroying Satan. The good people will then populate the earth, which will be ruled by the Government of God. All earthly governments are meaningless to Jehovah's Witnesses, so they do not serve in the military, pledge the flag, participate in political activity, and so forth. Their gathering place is called a Kingdom Hall, and their services focus on baptism and the Last Supper. Part of their individual mission is to spread the word through the use of their publications, often distributed door-to-door.

Judaism. Moses was crucial to the development of Judaism, through his establishment of various rights, such as property rights, and a day of rest. Another part of the code of Moses said that social justice is one way of expressing love for your fellow man as well as your love for God. The belief is that God is one, is omnipotent and omniscient, is merciful and loving, and God is there when you need him. Jewish people believe that because of this assignment to secure social justice, they have a heavier burden than other people. By following the Torah, one can learn what God expects of you. Judaism holds that unless you live your beliefs, you are not practicing your faith. The Reform branch uses English at its services, and has contemporary services, whereas the Orthodox branch, which was created in the United States as a reaction to the Reform branch, keeps the kosher laws and strict Sabbath, adheres to traditions such as separating men and women, and uses Hebrew. The Conservative branch uses both English and Hebrew, does not separate men and women, emphasizes modern education, and still believes in covered heads during worship.

Latter-Day Saints (Mormons). The Church of Jesus Christ of Latter-Day Saints was founded in 1830 by Joseph Smith (1805–1844) after visions he had, telling him that established churches were not teaching the whole gospel. The missing parts of the gospel would be revealed to him in the form of gold plates, which held the words of the Book of Mormon. Smith translated the plates, which he found, and began to send out missionaries. As the group grew, there were splits over issues such as polygamy. Mormons believe Christ will rule the earth. Mormons follow very traditional gender roles, with only men having governing power within the church.

Lutheran. Most dominant in western Europe, the Lutheran faith was founded on the teachings of Martin Luther (1483-1546). Lutherans are Christians who believe the Old and New Testaments contain all the rules for life. At their services, bread and wine are used, and they believe that those who take the communion take in the real body and blood of Jesus Christ. Christ is humanity's only savior. The Lord's supper is central to services, but each church creates its own form of worship; singing and preaching are also very important. There are shades of difference between various Lutheran sects, depending on which country initially influenced that sect. The minister of each church is selected by that congregation. The Evangelical Lutheran Church is liberal, and is in favor of the ordination of women. The Lutheran Church Missouri Synod is conservative and opposes the ordination of women.

Methodist. John Wesley (1703-1791), a Church of England minister, founded Methodism, so the influence of that church has been present in Methodism over the years. Methodists believe in the Trinity, the fall of man, the human need to repent, free will, and the Bible for one's salvation. The service may be as grand as the Anglican, or a much simpler one, depending on the individual church. The emphasis is on piety and religious experience instead of on doctrine.

Presbyterian. John Calvin (1509-1564) and others founded this church in Great Britain and Europe. He believed that those who are "saved" are chosen ahead of time, are predestined to enter heaven; good works will not get you there. What is unknown is exactly who has already been chosen. Christ represents salvation. The presbyters, or elders, ordain ministerial candidates.

Unitarian Universalism. This church was founded when the Unitarians and Universalists merged in 1961. Both can be traced back to at least the 1700s. "Unitarian" refers to the belief in one God, not in a trinity; and "universalist" means that anyone and everyone can be "saved." Unitarian Universalists believe each being is part of an interconnecting web of life. There are variations within the church, from Christians to atheists, but all are accepted as there is no central creed that is imposed on members. One former motto is "To question is the answer." Laypeople choose their own ministers, and their own order of service. Unitarian Universalism is considered a liberal church, and is very active in social causes. Women can serve as ministers.

Summary

Obviously, the list above is not exhaustive. There are many other faiths to explore. Some not described here are Pentecostal, Assembly of God, Hinduism, Buddhism, Amish, New Age, Native American, and others often called cults, such as Scientology or EST or Unification.

Finally, in looking for a new church and religion, two more

key questions to ask yourself are, "Do I feel better having gone to that service?" and "Will having attended this service make a positive difference in my life in the week ahead?" By talking to people, and by visiting churches when they have a regular service, only you can answer these for yourself.

9

Telling Your Family
You're No Longer Catholic

Q. 250: What does the fourth commandment forbid?

Answer: The fourth commandment forbids disrespect, unkindness, and disobedience to our parents and lawful superiors.
— *The New Baltimore Catechism* (p. 110)

Telling your family, especially your parents, that you no longer attend a Catholic church—especially if you now attend church in another denomination—is an event loaded with emotion. Catholic parents are taught that they are responsible for their children practicing the faith. So news that their daughter doesn't attend mass any longer, and may even be attending another denomination's church, is greeted with fear, anger, and disappointment; also, there is often an overwhelming sense of failure on the part of the mother because the church has traditionally designated her as the caretaker of the family's spiritual life. Phyllis, the restaurateur in Ohio, remembers, "My mother always told us that she would be a failure as a parent if we were not good Catholics." Fran says that in high school she " 'played the part' of a good Catholic girl . . . and eagerly awaited my college years so I could stop practicing the faith without having to deal with my mother."

Is it any wonder that many women leaving the church, who have been raised to be "good Catholic girls," keep their decision a secret from their families? Phyllis also says, "I was so afraid of hurting my mother . . . that when I married, we were married before a judge; we then went to some church in that city and took a bunch of pictures and sent them to my mother telling her this was the wedding. To this day (thirteen years later) she still thinks I was married in that church."

In a workshop I call "Telling Your Family You're No Longer Catholic," participants discuss these issues. At the beginning of the workshop, which has been attended by women and men in their twenties through their fifties, I ask, "How many of you have told your parents already?" and 75 percent or more raise their hands. So why are they there?

It turns out that of the attendees who raise their hands, about one-third are really there to hear what other ex-Catholics have to say. Another third are there because they have not overtly and clearly "come out" but have dropped frequent and broad hints about no religion or a new religion. The remaining third who raise their hands say they've told their families but the families are in denial about it, fully expecting, for example, that their daughter will "come to her senses" and rejoin them in the Catholic church one magical day, even though the daughter is a choir leader or governing board member in her new church, or even though the grandchildren are active and happy in the new Sunday school.

The booklet *Coming Out to Your Parents*, published in 1984 by the Parents and Friends of Lesbians and Gays (PFLAG), is a guide I use as the structure for the core part of these workshops.

PFLAG maintains that "coming out" as a gay person represents separation and loss to the family of that person; the booklet is based on work by Elizabeth Kubler-Ross, who, in studying death, grief, and loss, has defined the stages of understanding one goes through in coping with that loss. I have adapted PFLAG's material to this workshop, and it works well because the ex-Catholic's family can go through these same steps.

The attendees also use the phrase "coming out" because the impact of telling your parents that you're no longer Catholic is often as deeply emotional within a Catholic family as it is for gays or lesbians who come out to their parents about being homosexual. I do wish to add that outside the family, the ex-Catholic does not face the risks that the out gay person does, which makes the gay person's decision doubly hazardous.

One of the first things that we do in the workshop is to talk about "what" we each are now, in the religious or spiritual sense. Reaffirming the good things your new religion gives you firms the foundation of your decision to tell your parents about it.

As I review the stages your family may experience if you tell them you are no longer Catholic—and you may decide the best course is not to come out—I'll use the term "parents" to also mean "family." Also, the process can take them a few hours or a few years. Last, I would recommend that you tell them you're no longer Catholic not out of anger, but out of love. Anger may have sparked your leaving the church, but acting out of love will guide you to be patient and understanding with your parents as they take in what you're telling them. This process is a two-way street: they have a lot to absorb from you, and you must be patient with them.

The method in which you give this news can vary: face-to-face, on the phone, in a letter. It will depend on what you think will work best.

My own "coming out" was in the form of a letter to my mother, who lives in another part of the country. She and I have rarely seen eye-to-eye on any subject, and our self-expressive ways conflict readily. Thus, I chose this less-than-confrontational method, one that allowed her to react in her own time. In the middle of the letter, I told her about my new religion. (She already knew I hadn't gone to mass in years.) My words were, "I am telling you this because my new church makes me happy, and I can't hide my happiness from you. I know this hurts, but I don't think you'd want me to hide what makes me happy."

She never reacted directly to the news. She never mentioned the letter. For a while, I wondered if she'd even received it, and almost asked, but decided to let her tell me. Several months later, in a telephone conversation, she said, "I'm sending you some of these craft items I've just made. Maybe the ladies at your church can use the ideas for their next yard sale." She had, indeed, reacted in her own way, in her own time. And my point got across without the usual sparks.

The women in their survey responses have their stories. They talk about the costs of being honest, and the rewards.

Stage One: Shock

You've probably been an ex-Catholic for some time, and are comfortable with this status, but to your parents, this will be news. On some level, they may already have some sense of this anyway: you do not have a Blessed Mother statue anywhere in your home, or you make excuses about not joining them for mass, or you do not talk about your priest or your parish. Years before

I wrote the letter to my widowed mother, I sat down with my parents face to face, and told them that I would no longer be going to church with them. They told me they already knew "because you have no crucifixes in your apartment." It was actually hearing me say, "I just can't go to mass with you, church makes me so angry" that was the hard part for them. Words like "hurt," which is addressed later in this chapter, hung in the air. Now it was out in the open. But those Sunday morning knots in my stomach were gone. They were replaced by the kind of sadness that major change creates, but all of us seemed to feel relief that an unspoken, stagnant tension was gone.

This kind of moment between parents and children (of any age) is a defining one. The child says, "I am different from you, Mom and Dad. I am finding my own way." The parent thinks, "Is *this* my daughter?" A minority of "devoutly Catholic" parents are accepting, but usually those workshop participants who cannot bring themselves to "come out" have parents or families who are condemning when someone in the family does not follow the expected path. After all, by saying "I've found a new religion," a grown child is making the parent question how they raised that child, especially since, along with church expectations of parents in raising their children as Catholic, the Catholic church teaches that it is the only true church.

The message can take hours, weeks, or months to sink in. And each parent may be in a different place: your mother may resolve this for herself while your father may be still stuck in shock or denial for some time. Throughout, it helps to reassure your parents that you love them, or that they did their best for you, and that you only want to be honest with them.

Stage Two: Denial

Often the established family dynamic—how each family member relates with the others—which has long been in place, blames others for causing pain within the family. The family sees the parting not as a theological development but as an act of disobedience, betrayal, or deliberate hurt, caused by influences outside the family that they would call "enemies of the church" or "anti-Catholic." This hostility is a form of denial. It allows the parents to believe that the family is intact, that nothing has changed. It couldn't possibly be that our daughter has a mind of her own, is the underlying thinking. And if it's not our daughter who's caused this problem, it has nothing to do with us causing the problem.

Denial can also take the form of rejection that is expressed as "it's-only-a-stage-you're-going-through." Phyllis speaks again: "Serving on the governing board of our Unitarian fellowship, I was pleased (and worried) when my mother came to visit, for I was determined to take her with me to our church. She attended and took with her our newsletter, which lists me as serving on the board.

"Later at holiday time, she asked me if I would be going to the Unitarian Fellowship for Christmas; I told her 'No, we don't meet on Christmas Day because . . . so many of our members are traveling at that time.' 'Thank God,' she said, 'now you can go to your own church.' "

Jeanne's parents "view me as the 'black sheep' and have never forgiven me for leaving their 'perfect' faith. Even this past Easter I received a note from my mother reminding me that I should put 'God' back into my life." Jeanne, a forty-nine-year-old widow in Colorado with two children, resents this rejection: "I despise their God, . . . their outmoded beliefs, their unconcern for a search for truth, and most of all for not accepting me as a unique human being that simply doesn't believe in the Catholic church." While it's difficult to contain your anger when you've had such rejection, it is important to control it, and to channel the energy into building your new life.

Another form of denial is called noncaring. How did Maureen's family react? "Come on, they almost died! Momma taught me right from wrong and so I went wrong, yes? It wasn't her fault, my converting [to Judaism], yet she still loved me and ignored what was going to happen to me in hell. . . . She never talked about it. It didn't exist." Maureen's mother first reacted with loud hostility, then with quiet noncaring, or ignoring the reality she did not want to accept. Maureen was content with that solution.

Denial can also be a nonregistering reaction, or, "How nice, dear; now where should I put my new lamp?" Joan's parents "seem to look the other way. Very little is said, as if my non-participation does not exist if it is not acknowledged. . . . We attend a Unity Church of Christianity, a metaphysical church." Joan is thirty-five, divorced with two children, and is a computer operator in Ohio.

You will wonder if you were misunderstood, if they thought you were saying something else. Wait for an opportune time to bring it up again. After all, this is something important to you.

Denial is a coping mechanism. Go ahead with your life, but be patient with your parents. And be sensitive. When the opportunity arises—we women have been socialized to be good at sensing when the time is right—you can tell them more. But now is not the time to turn into a cheerleader for your new church, if you have one, or to attack the Catholic church. If you're not using your "ex" status as a weapon, you can afford to be generous here; after all, haven't you just done the most freeing thing for yourself in a long time?

Stage Three: Guilt

Your parents may be thinking that you left the church because of some small, correctable incident.

An elderly woman next to me at a Woolworth's lunch counter, where we'd both sought refuge on a cold afternoon, began talking with me. What began innocently as two strangers having polite conversation quickly turned into a tug of war when it became obvious that she was steering the conversation toward religion. One thing led to another, and she began recruiting me to come to her Catholic church. Rushing to finish my sandwich, I told her only enough to let her know I didn't share her feelings. "Oh, but so much has changed! Yes, there were one or two bad apples in the basket long ago, but the church has changed! Come back and see!"

The thinking here is that something needs to be fixed; that if only we, your family, could discover the *real* problem, we could patch it up, or apologize, and change you back into what you used to be.

Judging from what the women said in the earlier chapters about their reasons for leaving the church, the underlying problems are not simple and not fixable. The women address this topic—how the church must change—in the next chapter, but very few of them say any of the changes would bring them back.

Your parents' guilt, as a reaction to you coming out, comes in a few other forms. Another is in "what will the rest of the family think?" or "what will the church think?" Implicit is the lack of acceptance for you as you are. Maggie says, "I realized I was a feminist and become infamous for writing antiwar and pro-choice letters to the editor. My sister wrote that she never wanted to see me again and considered me dead. She is pro-life it seems. My mother waited a couple years and when I didn't shape up finally wrote that she wanted me to stop writing letters to the paper because it made her uncomfortable—'a lot of people here know who you are,' and suggested I volunteer to work in a hospice in order to help 'some poor human being' instead of, apparently, the 'poor human beings' where I *do* volunteer—a shelter for battered women. And I have done that for over ten years and she knows that."

Jimi's parents "were embarrassed . . . when I wrote from college to my old parish to tell them to stop sending me contribution envelopes in my name to my father."

This is a grave concern of your parents because they were charged with raising you to be a good Catholic. Maggie continues: "As a feminist I feel angry at my mother for her attempt at censoring me [from writing the letters to the editor]. I know my letters about religion, the pope, et cetera, she feels, reflect badly on what kind of Catholic mother she is."

Donna says, "My father believes he is going to hell because two of my sisters and myself do not go to church. He blames it on himself and no one can tell him elsewise. I feel sorry for him because he lives his life in fear of God and by the Catholic faith completely. He can never, never bend the rules for himself and everyone else who does bend is wrong. . . . My mother is very negative about sex, abortion, birth control, homosexuals, and people living together. She is not accepting of any of this and is very verbal about it. . . . My parents never question the Catholic ideas. They believe the pope's word is the ultimate law, and one should never have thoughts against it."

Once again, patience and information about "what" you are now—if they ask for it—will help. If you do not belong to another church, but instead can talk with them about your new beliefs, you can answer questions about what you're reading or meditating on. If you do belong to an organized church, and they are really curious, you can bring them to a social gathering of your new church members, or even to a service. Phil, an ex-Catholic friend who became a Unitarian, initiated his mother to his new religion by bringing her to a Sunday service in December. What he hadn't anticipated was that the minister's sermon would be titled "The Myth of Christmas." The sermon turned out to be tamer than its title. Phil's mother took it all in stride, and ended up telling Phil, "I knew you wouldn't bring my grandchildren into anything weird." Our parents can be more resilient than we think.

Stage Four: Feelings Are Expressed

Ricki remembers, when she told her parents she was no longer Catholic, "My mother was quite upset and my father often chastised me for 'hurting' my mother." It's at this stage of understanding that emotions come out. Often roles are reversed: your parents become the angry children, and you must be the patient parent.

Linda's grandmother overheard Linda say "that I had not been to the Catholic church for years but was currently attending services at Unity Church of Christianity. That set her right off. She sat there and told me that I was a satanist, a devil worshipper." The grandmother's irrational response is not all that unusual. Many Unitarians tell stories that their parents blurt out how upset they are "that now you're a moonie," the nickname for followers of the Unification church, which has no connection with the Unitarian Universalist church. At such emotional times, it is easy for your parents to be confused and believe far worse than anything that is real. You may wish you'd never said anything. But if they are letting out their feelings, they are moving forward. Weather the storm.

Ricki finishes her story: "My siblings gradually left the church, too, and my mother blamed me for 'setting a bad example.' " But, over time, "my mother seems to have come to terms with my/our leaving and while she wishes we still were involved, she seems to respect my decision."

Stage Five: Personal Decision Making

At this point, your parents are less emotional and have reached some reconciliation with your decisions. This may come in the form of support, as acceptance of your decisions.

Some of the women I surveyed reported a surprising reaction to their pronouncement that they were no longer Catholic: their parents agreed with them! Sometimes family members who are practicing Catholics feel as trapped by Catholic teachings as those leaving, and say so to those who are leaving or have left. I call this the "envious prisoner" syndrome, because those who are still "inside" openly admit they wish they could join you in leaving, but for a variety of reasons, they feel they cannot. They are the unhappy Catholics stuck in the Catholic Loop, the angry people on the train platform.

MaryAnn says, "My family is still Catholic and my mother regrets it. My sisters do not agree with all the doctrines either but do not leave. It seems to be okay [to stay] as long as you don't voice your opposing opinions, but I don't want to be that way. My oldest sister is suffering from many emotionally and mentally tormenting issues because of the Catholicism, in part, I feel. My other sister just goes her own way pretending and avoiding issues. They have not rejected me because of the religion."

Ronnie, the twenty-three-year-old psychotherapist in California, tells us, "I was last in my family to leave, so no big deal."

Some see this acceptance from family later on, when that family member has her or his own crisis. Victoria says her mother took the church's teachings very seriously but "became disgusted. At my father's funeral, my mother started screaming, 'Nonsense, it's all nonsense!' They had to shut her up."

Another type of "plateau" of this personal decision-making stage is one in which your parents let you know they just don't want to talk further about it. They don't want to be pushed.

Don't cut them off if they are at this point. Stay in touch with them; don't let them push you away. Mention your church or group from time to time, or introduce them to another church member.

A third decision is to wage warfare against you. Again, this may be only one parent or family member; they keep bringing it up, provoking arguments with you. They may threaten you with disowning you, for example; but this is probably not the first time you have heard this threat. They may insist on taking your children to CCD themselves.

One woman in one workshop spoke about her father-in-law, who continues to throw barbs at her, baiting her into defending her new church. She handles it by ignoring it, hoping fatigue will change his behavior. Sometimes that works—time is on your side. If your situation is like this, you may know another family member who can come to your aid, and that intercession may get the angry family member to be more reasonable. If nothing else works, your understanding that your decisions are threatening to this parent, and that is why she or he is nonaccepting, will have to suffice. You will need to turn to other people within your family for support.

Stage Six: True Acceptance

If parents understand within their own hearts that your decision is best for you, they have reached true acceptance. They may even defend your independence, taking pride in having shaped you to be so. But not every parent will get to this point. If they do, there is a sense of peace all around.

On Not Coming Out

When the "scale of pain" tips in the woman's favor—meaning, when the pain of keeping something a secret outweighs the pain a person fears of hurting people she loves—then being honest is an option she chooses. Maggie captures the essence of the conflict about coming out as an ex-Catholic: "As a mother myself I don't really want to hurt my mother. But I also know giving myself up will not win her approval."

It seems that when a person is assertive with her family in other parts of her life, it is easier for her to assert her own religious beliefs and practices. Indeed, it is difficult to break what may be a longstanding pattern of nonassertion with news that may be devastating.

Coming out assumes that the message is vitally important for you to give. It also assumes that you value *you* and that you think well enough of yourself to get yourself out of a miserable situation.

Nicole is forty yet is one who has not said anything to her parents. "As for my immediate family and relatives, they may suspect my not being a practicing Catholic. It is better they not know what my current beliefs are until they are ready. I just want them to know I am happier because of my religious enhancements."

Connie's mother "used to hound me about going to mass until I told her that if she worried about my soul to pray for me, but not to bring it up again." So Connie herself cut off any discussion.

Too often a woman says, "I put their feelings first." Like Phyllis, who sent wedding pictures taken in front of an unknown church, some women cope by lying. Dusty says she "still responds automatically '11:45' " when her mother asks her, every Monday morning, "What mass did you go to yesterday?" This may work for a while, especially if your parents live far away. But usually the lie gets deeper: next, do you send phony pictures of your son's first communion? All you're really doing is creating more pain for yourself.

If a woman consistently chooses others over herself in such important issues, she condemns herself to enduring a different kind of pain that only erodes her spirit—and her spirituality.

Taking the Family with Them

Women are leaders often without even knowing it, and "ordinary" women often make the strongest leaders. More than one movement has begun at the kitchen table, with the woman in the family saying, "This has to change"; then she changes something, takes the lead, and her family follows.

And so it seems when a family leaves a church: the women lead.

Maggie says, "When I left the Catholic church, so did my husband and kids." Lily "took my husband and four children out with me." Susan declares, "I led my family out of the church and into [a new church]." Glenna says, "We have all moved forward together."

Not Raising Your Children as Catholic

Exercise Question #4: "Angela decided to postpone the baptism
of her baby until her uncle comes home . . . two months [from
now]. What kind of sin is she guilty of, and why?"
— *The New Baltimore Catechism* (p. 144)

Catholic teaching has historically said that infants should be
baptized within one month of birth; indeed, some women in the
workshops remember being advised to have their newborns
baptized on the way home from the hospital!

Many inactive Catholics can ignore their conflicts with the
church until children come along. Many women and men in my
workshops say this event provides the first crisis for them as
former Catholics. Here is where they can no longer "hide" the
fact that they do not go to church; here their families no longer
look the other way. They must declare a position, otherwise they
will get lectures about limbo—or worse—from relatives or friends.
Paula, a waitress and mother of two, says she had her two children
baptized "because of other people making us feel guilty and
frightened at the thought of no baptism through the church."
Although the Catholic church has retired the concept of limbo—
a pleasant place where unbaptized babies get stuck for eternity—
old teachings die hard. And some of those teachings inspire fear.
Who doesn't remember Archie Bunker secretly baptizing his
grandson because Gloria and Mike no longer believe?

Many of the women surveyed and interviewed said they
would not raise their children as Catholic. Once again, sometimes
this is done openly, sometimes not.

Kelly "never had my fourth baby baptized and I swore that
no one would ever do to my children what had been done to
me. I raised them to question everything—look at the hidden

motive, read the small print, try not to get fooled because no one was a bigger fool than me. . . . Do you think for one minute that I want my sons or daughters within shouting distance of these poor misguided fools?"

Cyndy says that one day when she has children, they "will never be indoctrinated, as I was, that natural feelings and urges are sins that they will go to hell for, or should be punished for. My children will always know that they control their own lives; they must take responsibility for what happens to them, good and bad. My children will know that there are questions for which *no one* has the answer."

Terry maintains, "If I ever decided to have children, I would never raise them to be Catholics. Too much fear . . . too many contradictions . . . not enough compassion." Natalie agrees: "Catholicism is not conducive to a person's self-esteem or happiness. Of the five kids in my family, one or two are raising their kids Catholic . . . though they themselves don't go [to church]." Another woman says, "It is [my] experience that gives me the commitment to not impose Catholicism on my children. I find the religion depressing, demeaning, and insulting to children. They need to grow up 'freely' disciplined, not frightened and guilty."

"Catholicism is a bad trip for my kids emotionally and psychologically because of the guilt," says MaryAnn. "My oldest child, a son, went to a Catholic grade school briefly and was adversely affected by the constant emphasis on sin. My daughter went to kindergarten there and was discouraged from any but the 'helpmeet' roles." Another woman and her husband "do not feel it is helpful to put the burdens of religious bonds on our children. Why should they suffer through those agonies as we did? We raise our children as humanists and hope and believe they will find their own way."

"Raise my children as Catholic? *No!*" says Abby. "The church is archaic—it teaches intolerance and bigotry." Another woman believes, "Children raised Catholic aren't given the freedom to question their religion, nor are they given the chance to develop their acceptance of it. . . . Children are force-fed Catholic jargon, sometimes before they can say their ABCs. I think it's an injustice to a child to force any religion on them."

"I vowed I would never put my children through the awful things I went through," says Sara. "I sent my three girls to public school, not Catholic school." Yet Sara, who is not alone in her thinking on wanting her children to have some sort of religious training, sent her children to Catholic religious instruction (CCD), the only religion classes she knew about. But like her cohorts who sent their children to CCD classes, she didn't want them to have the same negative experiences she'd had. "Instead of religion classes every day like I had, they went only one hour a week. They were baptized, received communion, and were confirmed. That's where it ended; the rest is up to them. I exposed them because I think the church's code of ethics is a useful guideline for raising children. It is up to them to make the decision if they want to continue practicing their faith. [One] is twenty-one and is a nonbeliever right now. The twins are eighteen and still go to church. Whatever they decide is fine with me." She adds, "I'm glad I went the route I did [in leaving]. My children are happier and more emotionally balanced than I am, even after five years of counseling."

Rosalie of Oklahoma, too, "wants my thirteen-year-old daughter to have a religious identity, so we attend mass on occasion, but not enough for her to become a paranoid, needing-to-please-and-gain-approval-from-others type of person that I was."

May of Texas says her reaction to her own experience—to avoid anything to do with the Catholic church—shortchanged her children on religion. "All my children were baptized shortly

after birth, but none have received any religious education. . . .
I was so 'brainwashed' growing up that I didn't want them to
have to overcome the guilt, et cetera, caused by the indoctrination
I had. I do wish they had had some exposure [to religion], other
than occasional Sunday mass with my parents."

Others have made a clean break. Donna says, "My husband
was raised Congregationalist and we had our daughter baptized
that way." Glenna tells us that "each of my four children has
made his/her own religious choice. Even while I was still a
practicing Catholic I chose not to send my children to Catholic
school. The Catholic school I remember dealt heavily in fear,
and I was determined not to subject my children to any remnants
of that atmosphere that might have remained. I did take my
daughter and three sons faithfully to religious instructions while
they were in elementary school. None chose to remain in the
church. I am proud of them all."

10

Making Peace
with the Catholic Church

> Genuine forgiveness cannot be offered if anger and resentment
> are denied or ignored.
> > —Robin Casarjian, from *Forgiveness: A Bold Choice
> > for a Peaceful Heart* (p. 14)

Could it be that you—and the women here—had an *entirely*
negative experience with the Catholic church? Or was there
anything positive?

And would anything bring you—or them—back to the
Catholic church?

Before you say goodbye to something, you must say goodbye
to all of it, including anything positive. Once you recognize the
positives as well as the negatives, you can look at the whole
experience, "own it," finally put it behind you, and move on.
That is what this chapter is about.

In the last few years, many Catholic churches have been
holding programs urging "lapsed" Catholics to return to the fold.
The media have reported mixed results: some programs are

successful and continually bring inactive Catholics back into activity, others start out that way then dwindle down, and others fail to attract any participants. My limited knowledge of these programs suggests that the more successful are created for the returnees' needs, not for the church's needs.

Missing the Positives: Drama, Ritual, "Smells and Bells"

Dusty says, "What I miss is more about feelings and ceremonies than about religion. I used to sing in a choir . . . in an enormous Italian church when I was in high school. It was very emotional. I miss that. But it's not worth going for that 'high' to have to deal with being hurt by the bishop and the pope and everybody who treats me like I'm 'less' because I'm a woman, because I'm divorced. . . .

"Yesterday was Easter Sunday. I didn't go to mass. I walked along the beach, watched seagulls and waves and patterns in the sand. I felt very spiritual. When I bought flowers for my mother later that day, the smell of the lilies made me feel . . . homesick? For a moment at least. Homesick for the familiar. The glowing white vestments that followed six weeks of purple vestments. The smell of flowers mingled with incense. Children fidgeting in their Easter finery. Spirituality? Nothing like my solitary walk on the beach." The nostalgia Dusty is feeling here shows how intertwined her church past is with memories of childhood and home. Several of the women express this.

Loretta of New Hampshire "was very involved in the 'pomp and circumstance' of the church, and I now recognize the enormous beauty of the church's music and ceremonies. Catholic worship is truly rich in elegance and grace." Jennifer, now a Unitarian Universalist, says, "While I rejoice in Unitarianism, I sometimes regret that it is so plain. I bemoan the Unitarian ignorance about things liturgical. I am grateful that I have a sense of drama in worship. Nothing exceeds the drama of the host, raised in a slant of dust-moted sunshine, in a hushed cathedral. . . . I grew up with a sense of worship, a sense of the holy."

Cyndy, another now-Unitarian says, "There is only one thing that I miss from the Catholic church, its only good point. Ceremony and ritual are great forces. . . . I miss genuflecting and crossing myself. I miss kneeling, then standing, then sitting. I miss the little [responsive] phrases ('and also with you') and the long prayers that can be recited, over and over, from memory, without even thinking! I'm not sure that I want to make new decisions (I wrote my own wedding ceremony; do I have to write my own funeral?) every time something comes up. Sometimes it's nice to be able to go along with what was always done before. I don't always know what I'm supposed to do."

Susan sees "nothing positive about the church" for herself, but she adds that "people need ritual. Related to ritual is the strong power of the smell. Nothing smells like candlewax and incense." She refers to this as "smells and bells," and several of the other women also mentioned this phrase.

Other "positives" are more personal. Jill feels grateful that, "There have been individual nuns and priests who were very good to me. They taught me about the spiritual aspect of me, rather than centering on rules that I could never live by." Another woman feels positive about the church for the same reason: "It gave me a direction in my life when I was a very lonely child."

May would also agree. "I do value the religious education I had. It has made me the person I am today, and I feel that is good. I am a caring, loving person, but not the martyr that many women become. I guess all these years alone (no husband or live-in) has made me strong. I have kept the values and am going back to the morals I was raised with. We do come back to our roots. Mine were good, so I am happy with my circle."

One positive that Victoria remembers, growing up in the Bronx, was "when blacks were just moving in. My parish accepted them, and also integrated their schools before the public schools were integrated. I remember being proud of this."

MaryAnn "appreciated the emphasis on the atonement of Christ, on social justice issues, and the caring I did receive from a few individuals along the way who were being Christian in spite of the church."

But Myra is among those who feel nothing good about having been a Catholic. "I really don't feel anything positive about the church. I think the pomp of the pope, cardinals, etc., is so unnecessary."

Others who also thought they might come up with something positive but could not include Abby. There is "nothing positive about the church. It's got such basic flaws."

Phyllis agrees, seeing "nothing positive in the church. It is made up of a bunch of nonthinking people giving themselves over to males with overinflated egos. It is a total waste of time."

Kelly maintains, "I'm positive the priests have been pulling the wool over everyone's eyes for hundreds of years. Imagine. They drove around in their Cadillacs and had their allowances and their housekeepers and their fancy dinners and their drinks while next door, the nuns were washing, ironing, and doing penance, keeping silent."

Tina also answers about any positives, "Nothing, yet I long for the comfort of confession, that feeling when you are eight and know you have been loved and forgiven for what were then known to be definitive wrongs. But what would I confess now?

. . . What is left that can be uttered to a glass partition concealing a man I don't know? But viscerally, I long to experience the reconciliation."

The sacrament of confession is now called reconciliation within the church, and it means forgiveness for sins. Later in this chapter we'll address the yearning for reconciliation that Tina longs for. But our meaning will be, instead, in the women's forgiveness of the Roman Catholic church.

Would Anything Bring You Back?

This really has to do with why you left. If you left because of some particular incident, and you can now "forgive the church," it is far easier to return than if you are someone whose self-esteem was shattered or someone who cannot accept the theology that the church teaches.

Many of the surveyed women said nothing would ever bring them back to the Catholic church. Irene "will never go back to the Catholic faith. I have found theories of reincarnation and New Age philosophies to explain my 'why' questions more to my satisfaction." Jimi, in California, and a lesbian, says, "Nothing could ever bring me back to the church. I could not belong to *any* church. In my process of breaking with the church I became a convinced atheist. I realized that I had no knowledge of a god. All that [I thought] I 'knew' someone had told me—there was no reliable evidence."

Lily says, "Nothing, ever, would bring me back. I am not 'lapsed,' I am apostate." Victoria agrees but says, "Pope John XXIII was fabulous—maybe *he* could get me back!"

Glenna maintains that, "Nothing could induce me to return to the Catholic church although this is partly because my religious beliefs—finally formed on my own—would make me unfit for any Christian denomination."

Cyndy declares, "*Nothing* could ever bring me back to the institution that promotes the idea that women have one role, and men have a different role in society. *Nothing* could ever bring me back to the institution that believes in a male god. *Nothing* could ever bring me back to the institution that believes that women should not have the right to control their own bodies."

Annmarie observes that, "The church says . . . 'Sure we'll take you back as long as you follow our rules,' is the real message of the church" to gays like her.

"Would I ever go back?" asks Cathy. "No. I can't stand the guilt and judgements. I want to feel God's love, not fear my humanness. I want a religion that rejoices in God's word, Christ's action, and the strength of the Holy Spirit—I'm tired of feeling bad about my relationship with God and myself! Amen."

Kelly, Georgia, Abby, and MaryAnn all answered, "Nothing. Never."

Jennifer agrees. "I floundered around in no church for ten years, and then found a wonderful Methodist church that was, ironically, very Unitarian (although that was discovered only in hindsight). I told my parents after three years. They cut me off completely. I didn't even get a letter. They didn't mention my name [to others]. . . . My parents, although they are occasionally in touch, will never know about my Unitarianism."

Several of the women had comments such as: "Nothing comes to mind that would bring me back. I've grown. I'm not a scared kid anymore," and, "I never went back to the church but I pray now more than I ever did then." A third says she wouldn't go back because the church "has gotten too distorted and money-hungry for my tastes. The pope is too political and things are getting worse, not better."

Harriet, a word processor and single mother of two in Colorado, "can't defend the church's attitudes toward most social issues today. If I could, I would probably be a Catholic, still. The church contains great wisdom and beauty alongside indefensible closed-mindedness in areas other than the spiritual."

Others aren't so sure they wouldn't return. Loretta says, "I don't know if I'll ever become part of an organized religion again. I do hope I will successfully develop a loving relationship with myself which I think will lead to a loving relationship with that force, power, 'God,' that I only fleetingly begin to glimpse at times. Once I have arrived at some sense of balance, I would like to partake of group 'prayer' or 'worship,' and whether it will be in a Catholic church is yet to be determined. I tend to think not."

Anne "would go back if the church became less similar to a royal hierarchy (deacons, priests, bishops, cardinals, pope), and if they became less political, but I do not foresee this. I believe more and more people will leave the church to seek out a more humanistic religion."

Ronnie says, "I left the church because my pastor, a priest who had a position of influence on my life, left. He constantly encouraged us to think and to act on our thoughts and beliefs. A very traditional priest replaced him. . . . Focus was again on sin and evil rather than on justice and compassion.

"My new [Catholic] church saw God in every one of us, God not as a celestial being. My new church focused on the kingdom here on earth and how we have to work hard at it. If I found a [Catholic] community like this again, I might come back, especially if it encouraged questioning and growth."

Joan of Ohio wishes she could find a church like the one her parents attend. "My parents belong to a dynamic, fantastic parish outside of Cleveland. Their parish, in a comfortable suburb, does more than pay lip service to the needs of others, parishioners and non-parishioners alike. I truly wish I could find a dynamic parish like that near where I live. That involvement with the people means more to me than dogma. The two priests and the two pastoral nuns assigned to their parish are outstanding. They have numerous groups, a good education program, and serve God and His people in countless ways. The parish is progressive, embracing change and growth for all. I am tired of stodgy old parishes where the changes are all but ignored [and] women's roles are severely restricted, and even lay participation in the Liturgy and the parish workings is also restricted. These priests do not seem approachable, much like that one who merely told me to say three Hail Marys as if that would make everything right with the world."

Margo of Vermont admits that, "Even with all my bad memories, I feel a peacefulness in mass that I can't explain—and which frustrates me!"

Others are considering trying the church again.

Joan continues: "I stopped going to mass when I was nineteen and living alone. After about six years, I resumed going to church, but only for a year and a half. I drifted away gradually, working Sundays, with a small child, and later, a second child keeping me harried as a single parent. For the past eight years or so, I have rarely been to mass. Part of me wants to be active in the church, beyond the mass, especially on pro-life issues. Something was missing from my life, and as much as I wanted to become involved, there was something holding me back. . . .

"I am still drawn to the Catholic church, for all its problems. Eight months ago I attended a non-Catholic service (the first non-Catholic Sunday service in my life, having attended only a couple of non-Catholic funerals before). It was an ordeal. I didn't feel like I was in church. I have attended this Unity School of Christianity church for these eight months, and somehow, it still is not comfortable for me. My children like the Sunday school, and I have attended a class given in the evenings. I have read Unity literature and studied Unity philosophy for several years, and until recently, simply combined Unity philosophy with my Catholicism. I find much of Unity very helpful, very positive, very wonderful, but it doesn't have the impact of *the church*. The one, holy, Catholic, and apostolic church.

"I would like more information on current practices in the church, and I don't know where to begin to look for such information." Perhaps Joan has found a church that welcomes back inactive Catholics. "I am interested in metaphysics and New Age explorations, and I would like to see if there is any way to reconcile the philosophies of the New Age with the Catholic church. . . .

"At this point, I would really like to talk to someone in the church about what place, if any, I might have in the church. I have my two children, born out of wedlock, and I have married outside the church, as well as having a divorce in progress. I don't know if I *can* go back to the church." She adds: "I did find that responding to your survey helped me focus my introspection on areas of my lifestyle and philosophy which need work. I have been stimulated by this scribbling to check out area Catholic churches, and to see if there is a place for me in the Catholic church once again. Thank you for encouraging me to participate."

What Must They Change?

What must the church change in order for it to have a secure future? The women here offer free marketing advice to the church.

The church would say it must—and has—shifted its focus to the Third World. But Yolanda, a Boston-area woman whose family is from the Dominican Republic, sounds like many of the women here. She disagrees with the church on abortion and birth control, would not bring up any children as Catholics, and remembers that at her Catholic elementary school, "darker children were never chosen to be . . . in school plays nor in the church's choir."

But the church's optimism in these parts of the world may be short-lived. In Brazil, which is 75 percent Catholic, the birthrate has dropped from 5.75 children born to each Brazilian woman in 1970, to 2.35 in 1994. Fully 88 percent of respondents in a June 1994 survey of over 2,000 Brazilians said they do not follow church teachings on birth control and abortion. When women alone are surveyed, 90 percent of them say they ignore the church's teachings on birth control and abortion. These "limits to the reach of Rome" are also evident in that 30 percent of all pregnancies in Brazil are terminated each year by abortion (*Patriot Ledger*, September 3, 1994).

Several women say that the church must become more open-minded. Otherwise, Chris says, "there will be a steady increase of people leaving the church. And also, still fewer people will join the clergy. . . . On social and moral and sexual issues, it must make revisions or else Catholicism will run out of followers. Eventually the church will have to become more open-minded if it expects to survive."

Other comments include: the church must make "massive social changes—women in the priesthood; their views on abortion and birth control, homosexuality, and politics." "The future of the church is probably eventual . . . inclusion of other ideas and beliefs." Otherwise, they will face a "continued shortage of priests and nuns." "They may have to loosen up on some things—if they don't, they'll lose attendance, i.e., money, i.e., it would be tough for the priests and bishops to live the way they do." "The church must face issues not only of birth control, but divorce. . . . Mistakes are made in marriages. The church must be more responsive to the needs of people *today,* instead of trying to make everyone into little children just accepting whatever gets handed out to them."

Diane, the company controller in North Carolina, maintains that, "People aren't uneducated now like years ago. The hierarchy are so stupid. They are not trying to grow. Instead they are trying to hold the status quo for something that's outdated. They are still trying to dominate, instead of applying Christian principles."

Myra says the future of the church will be "that its population will dwindle to minorities who still believe in ritual and see things in black and white and no in-between areas. Such as the Mexican population who believe the man is the head of the house anyway." Another woman believes, "The patriarchal part of the church will eventually die, at least in the United States. It is critical that they open their eyes. They must meet the needs of women, the elderly, kids, young singles, young marrieds. . . . The church must know their needs and meet them." And, "The church needs to find more positive ways to emphasize the logic of leading a moral life, and to put more emphasis on family life being the responsibility of both husband and wife. Somehow, they need to find a little more respect for women as human beings, not brainless baby factories."

Some think that the Catholic church in the United States will go its own way. Ricki wonders "about the possibility of the church in the United States breaking from Rome. Another possibility is that new branches of the church will develop, without ties to Rome (instead of an actual, total break-off)."

Cyndy says the church "can't and won't change. The only future that I see for Catholic Americans is a breaking away from the Vatican. (The only thing that has prevented it so far is that Americans are so rich. The Vatican, I'm sure, would not want to lose out on those lucrative donations.)"

Darla is pessimistic. "So . . . knock your head against the church wall if you want to—but my advice is why bother. Shake the dust from your sandals and go to those who will hear you (advice previously taken from . . . Jesus of Nazareth)."

Changes affecting women must happen, several of the women say. Chris says, "Women will continue to realize how the church exploits them, and nuns will be almost nonexistent. So, the church will make an attempt to pacify women—and to sustain themselves—by allowing women to become priests. . . . First and foremost, the church must allow women to be equal in every aspect."

Lily maintains, "The church must begin to glorify women as creators of the race and the embodiment of the life principle. It must glorify and praise the sexuality of women as the most fundamental 'good.' The church must defend and protect the life-force of women with all its wealth and will. . . . If these things are not done, the church will choke to death on the blood of the womb which gave it life." As Lily describes this church versus women struggle, what she seems to be saying is that the church must extol women or it will die because women will leave it.

Geraldine believes that women will change the church. She asks, "How much longer this institution, the church, will have value to individuals . . . is a large question. I fear the answer is, for a very long time—depending, I think, on the world's women. . . . They (the laity) are as well-educated as their priests and nuns—and increasingly more competent and intelligent. . . . The church is in peril. Since Henry VIII and the [founding of the] Episcopalian church there is the fact that if Catholicism gave in on divorce, birth control, celibate clergy, and the subordinate position of women, it would simply be Episcopalian. . . . Wouldn't this mean a Protestant triumph? . . . The church is suited to times when very few people lived to be much older than forty, when one out of two children died before the age of two . . . and before tests revealed the same IQ distribution for females as well as males."

Debbie of Washington says, "I think you're going to see women more active in the church just as in the rest of society which is *slowly* changing. I am a career girl and I know in every area we are still pioneering the way for women, and yes, it is costing us. There are many struggles still ahead and women are going to have to continue to fight to make permanent changes."

If one looks to the new, 1994 Catholic catechism for signs of such change, little hope will be found. In the catechism's index, under "man" or "men" are 130 entries. But under "women" are only *five* entries.

But Connie still has faith that the men in the church can change it. "The church is an old institution and I feel sure it will survive in some form. . . . I've met some priests and one bishop . . . who I think are good, holy men and I've not always felt that in our clergy. I feel that it is men like these who will change the church, give it more meaning, have more understanding. . . . Change is what will keep the church intact, maybe not in my lifetime though." Perhaps these men *are* the church's only hope, given that women are not allowed to play a vital role.

Many women declare that the church must allow priests to marry, if it wants to survive. Glenna says, "To be a healthy church, I believe priests must be permitted to marry. Once the clergy has to live like the parishioners, I think the barriers will come down and attitudes toward sex and related issues will become more realistic. But this, for now, at least, is a fantasy.

I still become angry when the pope makes a pronouncement that could have been taken verbatim from the eighteenth century."

Others agree that priests must be able to marry. Polly says, "Denying priests and nuns the right to marry denies the human desire to share their lives with another. Besides, how the hell can a priest counsel a married couple when he has no such experience with that lifestyle himself? Choose celibacy if you want, but don't deny marriage." Another woman asks, "Why should priests remain unwed unless they choose to do so for very personal reasons? . . . We need spiritual leaders and they are the ones who have had the experience to advise and understand the humanness of mankind." And one more says the church "will fall apart unless they change" and "priests should be married so they'd know about life."

But Darla says "the possibility of making the church hierarchy more realistic is very, very remote. We tried. We saw Father Bob Duryea try by being secretly married for five years and having a son and wife live in another city, with the hope that if he could prove a married clergy could work, the Vatican would relax its laws on celibacy. He offered himself as a pioneer—tough luck, bucko—out he went!"

Kelly recommends certain changes but sees "the future of the church as that of a declining institution, an ancient dinosaur ruled by a befuddled Polish guy who thinks women should keep their mouths shut. In order to survive the church would have to take an immediate interest in human rights . . . as an institution . . . , not by just a few fervent individuals [within the church] who get their hands slapped when they speak up. Then priests would have to be allowed to marry so they could attract some normal people to the church. Of course, birth control would have to be allowed." But Kelly is pessimistic. "This is all pie-in-the-sky and will never happen so I can't conjecture a world where the Catholic church would be on the ball." Margo summarizes by saying, "As long as we have a traditional pope, nothing will change."

Cathy is among those who think the church should remember its roots. She believes "the Catholic church is caught in the same dilemma our TV networks are—ratings and revenue. The church policies come from the pope with various priests or dioceses changing them to fit the want (e.g., gay services). . . . There is too much confusion—too little commitment to the basic, original beliefs." Maybe she has something here: what a powerful change it would be if the pope, for example, visited a head of state, attired in a simple robe instead of his regalia.

Sara believes, "The biggest change [in the church] has to be that instead of being a money-making political power the church has to go back to being what it was designed to be—a holy place to find peace with God." She adds, "I think the way things are going, the church will destroy itself. More and more people are seeing what it has become and are leaving. Eventually the church will only be a shadow of what it is today."

Among the pessimistic is Holly, who believes, "The church will continue to exist as long as it continues to subjugate the minds of its people. Those people who need the rules and regulations in order to function will continue to carry the banner. Those of us who think, will leave. It is the epitome of the 'Old Boys' network. As long as the church can *control*, it will exist. It doesn't want people such as me—I ask too many questions—I *refuse* to be inferior, and I refuse to be considered *evil* because I'm female."

MaryAnn thinks "the church will continue to cooperate with some of the most evil systems in the world, as many other religions do, too. The church will not make any changes to defrock itself."

Maggie says, "the monolith exemplified by the Vatican cannot change and will eventually die. Women priests, married priests, the acceptance of artificial birth control, they can't accept these things and remain what they are—a man's church, run by men, for men. It is a church with a homosexual mind but one who at the same time considers homosexuality an 'intrinsic evil.' And women, of course, don't really qualify as 'real people' but only as a 'necessary' evil. This church will not, cannot, admit that it is sick."

Would the church listen to these women as they might listen to paid marketing consultants? All the above is free marketing advice. In summary, the women seem to think that in order to survive, the church must change so drastically—by ordaining women priests, by allowing priests to marry—that it wouldn't be what we think of as "the Catholic church" anymore. Could the men of the church hierarchy stand such changes? If one views the church as a business, the board of directors and the rest of the structure should listen to their customers—and former customers—if they want to keep the business going.

Making Peace with the Church by Making Peace with Yourself

There are many ways you can become at peace about leaving Catholicism behind. You may wish to express your feelings, from anger to regret, to a counselor or therapist. Or, you might talk about it at AA, in a support group, with your clergyperson, or with a friend. You could write a letter that you have no intention of sending, or you may express yourself through poetry or artwork. There are many self-help methods available today, several detailed in the work of counselors such as John Bradshaw, that help people let go of their hurtful past so they can live fuller lives. There are many helpful books out there that walk you through self-guided exercises that move you beyond anger.

The quote at the beginning of this chapter is a powerful one, and bears repeating: "Genuine forgiveness cannot be offered if anger and resentment are denied or ignored." The four chapters here that outline the four main reasons for leaving the Catholic church might have helped you express some of your own anger; in part, that is why the chapters are included here.

Why move beyond anger to forgiveness? Robin Casarjian cites several reasons.

> Forgiveness is *not* condoning negative, inappropriate behavior. . . . Abuse, violence, aggression, betrayal, and dishonesty are just some of the behaviors that may be completely unacceptable. . . . Forgiveness does not mean you approve or support the behavior that has caused you pain, nor does it preclude taking action to change a situation. . . . Forgiveness is *not* pretending everything is just fine when you feel it isn't. . . . Because being angry is frequently considered unacceptable (especially if you express your anger), many people learn early in life to replace genuine feelings with more acceptable feelings and behaviors. . . . *The most obvious reasons for forgiving is to relieve ourselves of the debilitating effects of chronic anger and resentment.* (pp. 12–15) [emphasis added]

Completing the survey for this book helped many of the women quoted here vent their anger. Until they wrote or taped their answers, these women had not expressed to anyone most of what you have read. So the act of sitting down at their kitchen tables, putting pen to paper or voice to tape, or meeting with me to be interviewed, was healing for many of them. Knowing their words may help you be as frank as they have been. It helped most of them get rid of their anger, freeing them to move forward.

Some samples: "Now when I sit in church, I don't feel so much hate and anger, because I know my opinions will finally be heard—and that others might find some help from them." "My gratitude is in knowing you have read this, and that others may read and benefit from your book. I can now let go of the past, and perhaps as a result, others who read my experiences may relate [to them] and let go of theirs." "Thank you for giving me an opportunity to get it off my chest. I was amazed at how much anger I still have. This is a very emotional issue for me."

Whatever method you choose, it won't be easy. Jill said, "Writing this was an exercise in my emotional strength. For that reason I am sending it as it was done—written in pencil on notebook paper." Another woman looked at my letter "for several days now. I am afraid of it. I have such intense hatred of priests and things 'Catholic' that I wonder how I could possibly stop myself once I get started." One woman said, "I hadn't realized until just now, talking about this to my roommate, how worked up your survey was getting me. . . . Being in AA I have been learning to get honest with myself. . . . Working on your survey . . . was making me feel guilt, shame, fear . . . but at the same time I feel relieved. My roommate suggested going through a lot of these issues . . . with a therapist. Maybe it's not a bad idea. I put a lot of this [mental] stuff away a long time ago." Another concurred, "This has been traumatic to write. . . . I feel better though! . . . Thank you for doing this!"

Others used phrases like "cathartic" and "emotionally purging." One can sense their relief. Now they can put their experiences behind them, and grow. Expressing your feelings, as these women have, will only clarify them, and will be the first step to moving on.

"Moving on" puts you in control. Loretta gives us a good example of this. "Just yesterday, as I rode in a subway in

Boston . . . I saw an ad by the Franciscan Friars inviting people who felt 'separated from the Catholic Church' for [any] variety of reasons to drop into their center. I was momentarily tempted to bring my new, liberated self there to have a discussion—but quickly recognized this as a residue of unresolved anger and dismissed the notion very quickly. This is not a battle I choose to enter."

Perhaps Martha sums up "moving on" the best: "I saw how much emotional energy my anger toward the church consumed— and that it had produced nothing in the way of positive change, other than to prompt me, finally, to salvage my heart by leaving. When I made the conscious decision to stop being angry at at the church, to really leave it, I suddenly had at my disposal the energy to pursue other things in life that have brought me the joy and the deep sense of peace for which I longed."

Part of learning to express anger and resentment, and for-giveness of something or someone else, is learning how to for-give *yourself*. As you read the women's words earlier in this book, many castigate themselves for "believing for so long," as if they had any control over what was foisted upon them. By forgiving yourself, you can eventually eliminate that ever-critical, church-instilled, self-doubting voice you carry with you. Again: only after you forgive will you be able to grow.

Forgiveness is what I felt at the Grand Canyon. I translated that forgiveness feeling as "God," which, for me, means "being part of something bigger than myself." The forgiveness I felt there was so grand that it swept any doubts and faults I felt about myself into the canyon wind like so many scraps of paper. In that same way, it taught me to accept my human frailties. And in accepting them as part of myself, that "forgiving force" nudged me to shed them or change them. Finally, I felt whole. And finally able to move forward.

11

Happy Endings and Moving On: From Here, Where To?

Deep down, where what I am today and what I yet may be
has always existed, there was a spirit, looking not for freedom
from religion, but freedom *for* religion.
                                    —from Jennifer's "Affirmation"

From here, where to, emotionally and spiritually?

Some of the women's words that follow answer a question
I asked them approximately three years after their response to
the initial survey. I wanted to know what other changes they
may have made, and I wanted to know what peace they may
have found in their lives after leaving the Catholic church. The
specific question was, "If you had to write a 'happy ending' to
your story of leaving the Catholic church, what would it be?"
(Note: several of the women who responded to this question as
well as to the initial survey saw the ad for the survey in a
Unitarian Universalist publication, thus the disproportionately
high number of responses that mention Unitarian Universalism.)

The women here who have chosen another denomination are

happy with their new church. Many are content not to go to any church. And others are still exploring. Once again, their words speak for themselves.

Their New Religions

Abby tells us, "In 1983 I became a Unitarian Universalist. . . . I watch UU kids being free and happy and themselves. . . . 'Cakes for the Queen of Heaven' [the women's theology seminar series] is excellent; it helps women look at their religious experience and puts back together a positive image of women. . . .

"I have found my church home in the Unitarian Universalist denomination. I feel a true sense of spirituality, not one based on meaningless dogma or sexist principles. I am active in my church, a member of the executive committee and the religious education committee. I teach a course in feminist theology each fall.

"I continue to be part of a women's feminist spirituality circle, and continue to teach not only 'Cakes' but also 'Rise Up and Call Her Name,' a curriculum that looks at feminist deity from all over the world. I now take female ideas and female deities and incorporate those ideas into my daily life. I especially enjoy leading the lay services at my church. . . . This church fosters that personal quest to find out what's spiritual to you. . . .

"I meditate, I do readings and poetry that is earth-based and in touch with nature. I see my work as a therapist as being part of a connection with people; this has a spiritual flavor to it. . . .

"I don't know what could be more spiritual than being connected with other human beings. . . . The human parts of you are the spiritual parts of you. . . . My faith today is based on being the best person I can be, on working toward the betterment of all humans. . . . I feel very whole in my spirituality. This wouldn't have happened if I'd not rejected the Catholic church. I'm just so happy I did not try to live as a Catholic, attempting to explain the hypocrisy and understand the contradictions all my life. I feel real sorrow for the truly spiritual women who continue to struggle within the church despite the dogma that keeps women in a lower status."

Carmen, another Unitarian, does "not go to church thinking that we all share a common dogma. Everyone has their own personal interpretations of how to believe. I have studied with the Rosicrucians in the past, and probably will either take the 'Course in Miracles' at a later date, or study again with a metaphysical group like the Religious Science group here."

Carmen credits the Catholic church with helping to mold her concept of God. "The Catholic church was a very good influence . . . in bringing into reality the very idea of God-omnipresence, of the source of all things, in ways that I see now helped me when I was living with my parents in a dysfunctional household. And to have hope and to persevere, and especially now and since the times we have lost our three children, ages nine weeks, ten years, and thirteen years.

"Perhaps I'm just a rather metaphysical person religiously, but even my early fanatic, zealous . . . Catholic self helped to solidify the basic structure of a Higher Power—and give me a real sense of other dimensions, of a way to self-actualize regarding my religious beliefs when I was older and which has brought me so firmly to the place where my religious nature resides now, i.e., that each one of us has a path to God within ourselves, even though there are many different paths. It seems important to me that I grow closer to God's force throughout my life."

Maggie, whose words end chapter 4, says, "I am now a member of a Unitarian Universalist Fellowship and hope to remain so for the rest of my life. What a comforting, supportive religion! Have you seen the button that says 'Patriarchal religions are evil'? To me, that says it all. How can anyone love a God that saves 'you' while the bulk of humanity supposedly goes to hell or their souls are extinguished? What comfort is that? A God like that, I prefer no God at all! If 'God' is not love, and I honestly don't see that the God of the Bible and the majority of organized religions is, I prefer no God. . . . I see religion as the enemy of all people and especially women!

"I like myself more and more as I get older. I like that I am a feminist, an activist, and a thinker. I am so lucky!"

Tillie, a married mother of three in Massachusetts, recounts that she has "been a Unitarian since 1970 and still think it's wonderful! . . . The intellectual level of the sermons is wonderful. No comparison [to Catholic sermons]! Here in the Boston area, Catholic churches are *big*. You could belong for *years* without ever making a friend—or even knowing the person next to you. Our Unitarian church is like a *family*. . . . I enjoy being part of a smaller group where I know everyone and vice versa. . . .

"I suffered a great deal as a Catholic trying to abide by the church's rules, e.g., birth control. . . .

"In short, I'm more than happy with my decision and only wish that I'd been able to make it much sooner. . . . My extensive reading (and some help from my husband) enabled me to 'break the chains' and find intellectual freedom finally."

Glenna notes that, "Even after ten years of freedom from the oppressive guilt- and fear-ridden Catholic church, I experience a sense of relief when I am faced with a difficult situation and can rely on my intelligence and common sense to make a decision. . . . Now . . . I am profoundly happy as a Unitarian. I have accepted myself as I am, and I am pleased with what I have found. I waste no time trying to find explanations for humankind, who are capable of great virtue and great cruelty. They just are. I find more wonder in the natural world than there was in the supernatural world of the religion in which I was raised." Glenna adds, "I can now enjoy my memories of a childhood that was enriched by the ritual and security of the religion; but I am free of the fear, guilt, and archaic dogma that adversely affected my young adult years. I still get a rush of relief when I read about some new idiotic and infuriating pronouncement by the pope and realize that I am personally unaffected by it. I think of myself as a 'born again agnostic.' "

Susan of Michigan says her happy ending is "that I finally feel after all these years that I am a 'recovering Catholic.' My twelve-step program for recovery includes participating in the Unitarian Universalist church. . . . I belong to a women's group where many of the women are also recovering Catholics. We develop and participate in rituals that honor our pasts, 'presence,' and futures. As a psychotherapist about 90 percent of my clients are or have been Catholic. I am urging them to share their stories, design their own rituals, count on their *own* integrity, and be in charge of their own spirituality (whether or not they remain Catholic). I also help them find gentle priests who understand women's issues like abortion if they continue to desire 'forgiveness' for their 'sins.' . . .

"I have graduated from the University of Michigan with a degree in social work. I continue to work in therapy to remember and work through the abuse. . . . I'm on antidepressants and feel good and not guilty about that. . . . I've done bioenergetics for about two years, do journaling, art therapy, daily meditation—all to stay sane and push away the guilt and shame. I've participated in many workshops, including 'Saint John Bradshaw,' to help erase the messages that I am bad.

But she speaks of scars. "I live a life many would covet—

a nice husband and home, wonderful grown kids and all. I'm well respected by other professionals and have many friends. But underneath it all is the constant struggle, the $10-12,000 a year for therapy, the guilt, the shame, the sleepless nights, and before I get up to speak to an individual or a group . . . I always hear my eleventh-grade nun admonishing, 'Who are you with your little mind to question the great minds of the great men of the Church?' " Susan answers triumphantly: "I do it anyway!"

Like Susan, MaryAnn is involved in a twelve-step program that has helped her. She is an elder in a Unitarian church but, "I find more of the ideal of the church I am looking for in my twelve-step program (modeled after AA)." And today she gains strength from being a Christian Unitarian. "Since my former husband was a black minister who emphasized the Bible for his purposes, I was steeped in that, too. Through it all, my relationship with Christ has always rescued me and strengthened me. I don't think anyone or any church in the world can take that away from me. I feel that I am personally, spiritually indestructable, and eternal. There have been several mystical and spiritual experiences such as dreams and visions which have helped me through the years. If a religion does not promote healthy, positive personal and social development and does not enable people to stop misusing one another, I don't think it is in harmony with God's will for us." MaryAnn's "happy ending" is "that the inner trauma and intellectual striving I had to do to become free of the subtle and insidious emotional and mental crippling that the church affected me with, has fortified me in a deep and precise way against other systems which attempt to control and manipulate people through guilt, fear, and intimidation. My relationship with Christ is now based on the knowledge that he desires my fullest development and does not desire my death or demand that I rejoice in suffering or pain."

Anita's spirituality has blossomed since the day she served as a substitute altar boy when she was a girl, only to learn she could never really fulfill that role or any other she wanted within the Catholic church. "In taking back my spiritual power, I find both the questions and the answers, the mystery and the power in myself, where they have been hiding all along. I am still angry, but now I am using that anger to fuel my writing, to keep me aware of where I'm giving my power away again, and to keep me open to that small voice inside that is God for me. I reclaimed my spirituality, and the positive aspects of my Catholic upbring- ing which included a sense of mystery and the importance of ritual in spirituality. I am now a director of religious education at a Unitarian Universalist church, a member of a women and religion group, and a poet who delves into the spiritual in every aspect of life."

Darla describes herself today as "agnostic, [and] my husband says he is atheist and our [three] children do too. I like the Uni- tarian congregation because I'm OK, you're OK. . . . One pamphlet I remember very well from Catholic church was called *They Threw Out Confession and Replaced It with Psychology,* as if that is a bad thing. But when you think about it, that's the best thing that could happen. Weren't we asking our priests to be our guides and psychologists?" She speaks of a priest, years before, who asked the parishioners during a sermon, "What will be the role of a priest in the future? Why do you need a priest?" She says, "That same priest has sought and found a meaningful life elsewhere than in the church. So have we." Darla's "happy ending" is: "Freedom! The bonds that held me so tightly are gone, I am free to choose to be a good person—my choice, no threats of hell and sin and punishment on earth. I still thank 'God'— whoever or whatever—for the blessings in life and ask for help in troubled times. But I have new faith in myself; I have to do what is right and good for me and the world. I take immense pleasure in knowing I'm doing this because I want to."

Natalie, also Unitarian Universalist, notes "my oldest sister is a Protestant, and my youngest brother goes to the Buddhist temple with his wife and daughter."

Jennifer's journey brought her to Unitarian Universalism. "I feel religiously fulfilled now for the first time in my life. I began attending my . . . Unitarian church in St. Louis in 1984. I sing in the choir, am on the board of trustees, and have conducted summer services for three years. Two years ago, I began publishing a Lenten meditation manual with contributions of original material from members of the congregation.

"There is no more conflict between religion and humanness. I have seriously considered the ministry, but have discarded the idea for now. The shadows of growing up Catholic have left too many scars for me to consider seminary at this point.

"I've found a permanent church home and have thought through my personal theology. It is an open-ended view, allowing for new revelations. I am spiritually at peace now."

Cyndy says, "Two years after I finally and permanently left the Catholic church . . . my mother introduced me to the Unitarian Universalist church. . . . Although she was not a member, when I told her that I just wished I could find a church that was not based upon the Bible (which I had decided was derogatory to women, capricious, and inconsistent), she knew where to steer me. I have finally found a church that I can believe in! I am highly active there now, and am currently chairman of the religious education [Sunday school] committee. . . . I don't have to be a hypocrite, or say things that I do not agree with. . . . Hopefully my children will also form a strong attachment to this wonderful church so that they will always have the sense of 'religion' that we all seem to need." Cyndy, like several of the other women here, reflects that, "The Catholic church has given me a deep sense of religion and spirituality which I utilize in my new church. . . .

"The priests and nuns who taught me, taught me well, and always bade me to have an open mind. I believe that when I originally wrote my answers to your survey I was still very angry. I am no longer. I have come to terms with myself, have found a wonderful new church, and still appreciate the history and sense of wonder that my original church gave me. My writing to you may have been cathartic and helped allow me to grow beyond my anger. Thank you.

"I have tried hard to extinguish the patriarchal image I have of God and replace it with a gender-neutral image of the force of life. Many women in my church have worked hard to worship a female Goddess instead of a male God, but I find one as bad as the other. The power that formed the universe and that forms the basis for all life should not be presented as if in the image of one small part of it. I think the human race is ready to accept that the power of creation is unknowable—and we should stop trying to put a face on it."

Several of the women are now Congregationalists (United Church of Christ). Margo says, "I joined a large Congregational church about two years ago. The formality and 'pomp' that I crave is there yet the *people* run the show. *We* choose the ministers. Along with our 'pastor' we chose a married couple, both ministers, to become the associates. All the ministers (three) preach about today's experiences and how we can grow in positive ways (as opposed to the Catholic fire and brimstone).

"I am 'at home' and very active in the church. I've studied theology . . . and my spirituality is alive and spirit-filled. I am whole because of my faith.

"I'm not saying any one church is perfect and my God has

not changed, just my worship. The ministers share their humanness and that helps me so much to know I am not alone. They are not on a pedestal. There are so many ex-Catholics in my present church, it's incredible! (It feels like old home week).

"Leaving the Catholic church is like a death in me. Every once in a while I think about the twelve years of Catholic schooling and forty years of being Catholic and for brief moments, I am saddened by 'what was.' Self-discipline is the only lesson I have learned and kept. The rest is history."

Beth, also, is now a member of a Congregational church. "It is youth-oriented," she says. "My first impression of this church was, 'No kneeling!' It's warm and healing, stressless, no guilt here."

Donna says, "I have been going to a Congregational church. I enjoy it because it allows me to have freedom to believe what I want and not be condemned for saying something that goes against the church's preaching. The Catholic church is so much of a dictatorship, it does not allow any freedom of speech, thought, or action. I have found a deep appreciation within the Congregational church for them allowing me to feel that I am okay, and will not be punished for believing what I feel is good for myself. At my church, women are ministers and are an active part of decision making. I want my children to see that religion is to be shared by all equally, and there is no division of women and men.

"I finally feel at peace with myself and believe I have done the best thing. My parents still do not understand my actions, and feel they have failed in a mission. I hope that someday they will accept that I am not a Catholic anymore, but I am still a good person within God's eyes."

Today, Maureen is Jewish because "the ethical concepts are good."

There are other, less well-known paths. Holly says, "My husband and I are members of the United Church of Religious Science (very similar to Unitarians). We are happy. I have no guilt (or almost none, but I have to work on it). My husband has gone from being a lifelong Catholic to being a student of metaphysics and Science of Mind with me. What made *him* change? We have two daughters, and when he realized what the church was telling *them* he began to reevaluate his thinking. I am so blessed with this man who is working with me to find answers. I'll never forget the day he turned to me and said, 'The pope is a fool.' Wow!"

Judy of Colorado attends "the Church of Religious Science whenever I feel like I want to attend a church service." She talks about her journey. "Al-Anon helped me grow up even more. It helped me know I could stop being a martyr . . . and it helped me expand my understanding of God. EST helped me take responsibility for my life and my choices and stop blaming the church, my family, etc. Science of Mind studies have helped my further growth, to know that I continually create my life and experiences." She adds, "I am now involved in a philosophy that believes we create our experiences by what we think and by what we believe. I know that the Catholic church fit my consciousness at the time and that the time I spent in the Catholic church was part of a process. None of it was wasted and I have no resentment or anger for the church. Any organization has its own set of rules and politics. Each group is seeking the Truth. The Catholic church is a path for many and it was my path for a while." Judy is only one of several women here who have mentioned alcohol addiction and AA as a way out ot it. Alcoholism seems to be intertwined with the women's unhappiness with Catholicism, based on the number of women who mention alcohol as a problem for them and/or their families.

After ten years as an agnostic Unitarian, Polly "embraced Christianity once again. I am now an Episcopal seminarian at Harvard Divinity School seeking ordination in that tradition."

Martha, who once studied to be a nun, says, "I am no longer a practicing Catholic. All of the fear and most of the guilt have faded into memory. What God thinks of me, I don't know. And that's okay. That's part of the freedom of being an Adult of God." Martha has married and become an Episcopalian. She writes with a sense of humor: "We are taking a 'long view' of our choice of church since we both want to raise our children in a Christian faith (so they'll have something to reject as teenagers!)." She adds that her husband "wanted a church wedding—he was raised a Lutheran—and I agreed so long as it wasn't a Roman Catholic church. . . . This [Episcopal] church appears to provide room for questioning and doubt. It also regularly involves lay men *and* women not only at the lectern but also at the altar during the celebration of mass. And there are *lots* of altar girls! It was quite a moment for me, the first time I received communion at this our newly adopted church. It was the first time I could say with real finality that I had *left* the Roman Catholic church. We both have hopes for spiritual growth through our new affiliation.

"Over the years since leaving the Roman Catholic church, I have learned to recognize the differences between religion and spirituality. Realizing that I could grow spiritually without necessarily involving myself in the trappings of religion was immensely freeing! . . .

"I now believe that God is essentially unknowable in that He/She/It is wholly Other. I do believe that Jesus was God's anointed and that he brought us extraordinary knowledge about our Creator. That knowledge . . . concerns the conduct of our lives here on earth. While Jesus spoke about many different things, I think that the thrust of his message is that the kingdom of heaven is here and now. And so is hell. It's not a matter of keeping individual scores during our earthly lifetimes in order to earn heavenly rewards or eternal damnation. . . . Our lives are interdependent. We can work to bring peace and joy to ourselves and others, or we can inflict pain on ourselves and others. Usually we do both, because the forces for both good and evil reside in each of us. I believe that if God is calling us to anything, it's to be co-creators with Him/Her/It. . . .

"I believe that life after death is like being a drop of water in a great ocean. The individual spirit or soul does not have a singular identity but, rather, merges into a vast oneness of being. . . .

"This church is not free of politics and power struggles, but it also does not look upon any one person or group of people as the ultimate authority. Here I can think for myself, make choices, express opinions without fear of reproach, expect to be treated with respect—in short, function as a responsible adult. . . . I 'have a voice and a choice.'

"Our daughter Katharine will be brought up as a Christian with, we hope, faith in herself, the courage to make her own choices, the ability to speak her heart and mind, and the freedom to seek God in whatever way is best for her—including even Roman Catholicism."

A Church of Their Own

Many of the women surveyed said they do not feel the need to go to church, and instead have a faith of their own. Each believes in her own way.

Dusty says, "What's so weird is that the further I get away from THE CHURCH, the more spiritual I feel. I feel less judged, and I feel like a good person. I do work that is fulfilling to me and is good for other people. I have two sons who are really aware of 'good' vs. 'evil,' that it has to do with loving themselves and loving their neighbor and not with whether they went to mass on a holy day or gave up candy for Lent." She has "discovered Creation Spirituality, ironically, through the teachings and writings of a priest, Matt Fox. When I read Matt's book *Original Blessing* last year, all the questions I had since I was eight were answered. The Cosmic Christ, hidden from me by the distortions of the power-centered patriarchal church, did—*does* exist! I can think of myself now as a 'visceral Catholic' in the *universal* sense of the word. I am studying the mystics and finding a deep feminist spirituality that I knew at a gut level when I walked on the beach. I am connecting with a community of people from all over who feel like I do. . . .

"I am hungry for more, more, more, instead of feeling starved! The irony of this is that if I hadn't been raised Catholic, been introduced to the Gospels, the rituals, the sacred music . . . I wouldn't have been able to connect to Creation Spirituality in the same way as I am now. (The seed was there under all the domination and rules and paranoia—amazing!)

"Every now and then I am still confronted by the stupidity of the authoritarian church—most notably last year at my father's funeral when the pastor refused to let us read stories written about my dad by his grandchildren and grandnieces/nephews, refused to allow my father's favorite hymn to be played, and refused to allow the family to select scripture readings, even from *approved* sources. I was angry about that (still am) but I'm able to look at it more as a corruption of power than as proof that the church stinks.

"I feel now that I'm on a spiritual journey that's stretched across a universal continuum—that the individual hurts I've experienced . . . are all part of the balancing act—it's what I do with those hurts—do they help me grow and seek peace and justice for all or do they make me shrivel up and deny my gift of life?"

Georgia "never believed in a benevolent God (I did believe in the one who used to scare me into trying to be 'good') and today I just believe in a large cosmic consciousness to which I feel we are all connected through love and in which we are all equal . . . co-creators." She adds, "I now feel free to make my own moral decisions. My spirituality goes far beyond that which is found within a strict set of artificial and outdated guidelines. Because I am not limited to conjuring up a display of religiosity on Sunday and holy days, I now make every day an event of spiritual meaning. By no longer adhering to the constraint of so-called holy places, I celebrate the divinity of all things in all places. I am a much better person for this."

Connie says, "Now we live the way we always have wanted to live. We hope we do the right (good) things, and that whatever God watches over us, understands." She whimsically says: "If I ever come back in another life (could be!) I might try Buddhism."

Kelly says her happy ending is that she is out of the church; she expresses horror over a spate of recent news stories about pederast priests, saying these stories "have convinced me that it was with God's blessing I was guided away from the church."

Victoria says, "The happy ending is the break with Catholicism and its anti-human or anti-humanistic strictures, its superstitious rather than truly moral restraints, and its burden of inane guilt. The church *has* improved, or at least there are admirable pockets of rebellion within it. If this had happened forty years ago, I might still be a Catholic. But lost faith, or the willing suspension of disbelief, cannot be regained. . . . I have no religion, no idea whether I believe in God or not. . . . A happy result of the happy ending is a happy marriage to a non-practicing Protestant husband."

"While God is very present in my life," says Jill, "I have eliminated the various rules we must live by."

Other women had these things to say: "Now I rely on myself for validation of my own self-worth. Another happy ending is that I now believe that whatever this 'God' thing turns out to be, that I am part of it. God to me is not something or someone separate to worship. God is me and everyone else. God is the whole of everything and I am part of the whole, therefore I am also God." "I found a way to worship God that is much more fulfilling to me than a stern patriarch forever saying no! In myself, I've found—a *force* that is both male *and* female and neither. I see that power in nature around me, and in other persons. I can rejoice in the fullness of my self and the world around me, concentrating on *becoming* instead of on guilt. I'm still working on this—reading, talking to other women, learning about myself— freeing myself from the bindings of '*not* thinking' that the Catholic church wrapped so tightly around me."

Adele is bisexual. She says, "I . . . could not join a church that did not embrace and accept people's sexuality. Thus I explored and left the Catholic faith, considered the Baha'i faith, and am now checking into the Unitarian Universalist faith. It *does* embrace diversity. The people seem like questioning, caring, and progressive individuals. I find this a refreshing change. Also, the services are less ritualistic and the minister is not removed or aloof."

Loretta says, "I am working on a spiritual relationship with 'something'—but I suspect that until I learn to totally love myself, I will be unable to make the 'connection' I seek. That notion reminds me of scriptural phrases I . . . heard paraphrased during my religious education ('you must love thyself'). There are many,

many ideas I heard during my Catholic years which are only now taking on a positive meaning. I think the basic message of the Catholic church when it came to a relationship with God was and is no different than those messages communicated by other types of religions, by twelve-step programs such as AA . . . , by poets and writers, by philosophers. . . . [I]t's the [Catholic] *delivery* that got me. The messages were given to me in the context of my not being worthy, and God being 'fatherly' and 'stern.' These messages have nothing to do with what I now think of as the spiritual aspects of life.

"I now believe there is no black or white. There is no 'all right' or 'all wrong.' There is only 'difference'—and a need for balance in everything having to do with living. I am trying to value the 'differences'—to become the best person I can become and to accept the me that I am as a worthy, loveable woman. Only then will I be able to love and accept everyone else. Even those misguided nuns and priests. . . .

"I have dismantled the old concept of 'God' and work now at developing an understanding of what I believe regarding a power greater than myself. My intellect constantly tells me a connection with such a force or power is possible, and my emotions tell me that I have a strong desire to foster such a connection. Integrating the three (mind, emotion, spirit) is providing me with the greatest challenge of my life. I suspect it will be a life-long journey."

Loretta adds, "My having left the Catholic church has resulted in my receiving a very special gift—I've found myself and within myself, a spiritual dimension. I now have an internal connection with something that I believe lives in everyone and everything. I suppose it's my new concept of 'god.' I've worked through a lot of my anger and can now 'see' that I do have worth, and that I am the one who defines what that means for me. I feel separated in a very healthy sense from rules, and church-type authoritarianism; free to determine and live by rules that are truly mine.

"*If* I ever join an organized religion again, it will be something . . . where *all* diversity is welcomed and men and women are viewed as equal and as having minds of their own."

Others who have not yet found "a home" have these things to say: "I am rather unhappy now that I have no church. I feel a need for spiritual direction. I still believe in a benevolent God, and hope to find a new church one day to fill my spiritual needs." One of the women is looking for "a God and a church who will understand, support, and encourage me in making my own decisions but who will also forgive me when I make human mistakes." "I have been experimenting with different churches. I feel a lot freer and independent." "I am still questioning. . . . Positive things have followed me through my life which have roots in my Catholic upbringing—such as the need to take time out to contemplate and organize my life. Rituals also continue to have value for me. I believe that life is sacred."

Some of the women clearly lean toward Christianity. For a while, Myra went to a Lutheran church, her father's denomination. "I do not attend a church at present. I consider myself a Christian with a personal relationship to God/Jesus, read the 'Good News' of the Bible, watch and listen to Pat Robertson— I find his TV ministry very inspiring. Although I do not 'belong' to the Catholic church, I find myself defending it . . . [to] a close relative who now belongs to a fundamentalist Baptist church. I still use a Catholic Bible. I never read the 'gloom and doom' of hell. I seldom read the Old Testament. I'm not sure right now if I sometime in the future again join the church if it changed more toward women, birth control, and priests being able to marry and have a family (so that so many wouldn't leave)."

Debbie says, "I am happy to feel free and well and know that in my heart, I love the Lord and that He does speak to me. I am set free from man-made boundaries to love and serve my Lord as I know Him! My view is that life is supposed to be a joyous celebration—and is that not why He died on the cross? For us? For us to live a certain type of life down here. For my own choice of religion, I have no affiliation with any particular church. I feel that the way you live is much more important than the weekly attendance of a ritual. I do a lot of reading about Asian religions that give me great insight and expand my spiritual horizons. In a way I enjoy going to [Catholic] church with my parents once in a while; it's nice to feel the community of belief around you, even if you don't feel yourself to be a part of it.

"On the other hand, I respect the teachings of Jesus. I feel that the highest spirituality is achieved in living a good life— respectful of other people and of the earth that it is our duty to care for. My sex life only affects me and is therefore no one's business but my own. As far as I know, Jesus never said anything about birth control, abortion, virginity, or male supremacy. He had many women friends and always treated them as intellectual equals. Indeed, Jesus may well have been scorned by many of today's devout, since he consorted with whores and other sinners."

Bobbie "married a Catholic who also did not attend services. . . . Two years into the marriage, we divorced. 'The ultimate sin.' (. . . We did have a Catholic wedding.) . . . I went through a hard time during the divorce and really needed the Lord. The first time in years. He answered, as always, and I gave myself to him. Since that time, I've never felt as religious and/or close to God. . . .

"I am now remarried . . . to a wonderful guy [also previously married and divorced] who was also brought up strict Catholic and was an altar boy. Now you can't get him into a church. He even speaks 'doubts' about God, which bothers me; but you cannot make someone believe until they are ready." Bobbie says, "I am closer than ever to God and he is now prayed to daily. When I was in the church, I followed 'their' repetitive routines and never really felt close to God. Now I've never felt closer to him and my life is so much better. God is precious, religion is not." She is now "interested in a nondenominational church. I want to go to God publicly, but I don't want to be judged by man. I know many people who have left the church. It is so wonderful to have God back in my life without feeling guilty."

Bernice says, "I am not filled with bitterness as so many other former Catholics are. . . . The faith I had as a Catholic girl has changed in some ways and been reinforced in others when I became a born-again Christian. I no longer trusted the Catholic church to make my decisions or tell me what to think or believe. However, I often attend Catholic service, though not every week. I have no problem with worshipping God in a Catholic church, but I worship him with a new heart. I also am free to attend interdenominational churches, to lift my arms and praise the Lord.

"I believe there is error in all churches and that churches are man-made, not God-made. I believe that was the message of the transfiguration when Jesus told the believers not to build temples to Him. Worship should be free and doesn't need a building. I carry Jesus in my heart. He is my personal Lord and Savior.

"In other words, I see the Body of Christ not as a denomination, but a group of believers who are scattered in different churches. Basically, they are joined by belief in Jesus Christ as Lord and Savior. We worship the same God, though some lift holy hands to the Lord and others kneel."

Annmarie calls herself "an active Christian living by the

Golden Rule, growing and helping other people grow to their full potential. New Age meditations feel right to me."

Others also find New Age spirituality fulfills their religious needs. Nicole summarizes her religious background for us, and talks about how New Age and metaphysical beliefs hold the future for her spirituality. She tells us her "background is a childhood of strong Catholic upbringing. Both of my parents (who are now divorced) are strictly Catholic, and so are their relatives. My sister married a Jehovah's Witness in the late '70s. My other four brothers married Catholic women; one of them is divorced.

"Throughout my child and adolescent years, I devoutly practiced the Catholic traditions. Later in the mid-1960s, I turned away from the church in disgust, frustration, and anger. Today, my husband and I do not practice any religious denomination, although he writes 'Catholic' when asked his religious preference on documents and I write 'no religious preference' on my documents. . . . I do not now denounce the Catholic system; I learned valuable lessons from its system. . . . My beliefs have satisfactorily expanded into metaphysical concepts and philosophy—and, with elevated emotional impact—my religious questions of the past and present are relieved of anxiety for the future. The many questions I asked of Catholic professionals in the past have been explained . . . while researching other religious denominations and finally accepting the metaphysical belief system." She found that in so many religions, "woman was subservient to man and to God. Her direct link to God would be prayer only; all other means were through man (i.e., communion, confessions). . . . My current beliefs . . . are unconditional to man or woman!

"Today I see the Catholic foundation struggling to keep the faith, while I continue to embrace a comforting status within my present belief system. . . . As a result, I am free from religious male oppression and am a happier Being relating to my inner concept of God. I'm a happier person with the freedom to roam through my spiritual needs without fear of damnation or death. By nature, I am gentle with all that encompasses Mother Nature and God's three-dimensional beauty of Life, and I respect the rights of others. My New Age beliefs enhance my understanding of human nature. . . . Miracles are not within the religious dogmas, but within the individual Soul as it evolves on its unique path to the Creator of All That Is! Having been a Catholic, I can compare my present spiritual Self with previous religious upbringing. I'm a more pleasurable and optimistic person. I am free!"

And Tina muses that, "Perhaps, I, as Tennyson describing his friend William Hallam, will come to 'fight the spectre of the mind and win.' I will find a stronger faith, my own."

Won't Go Into a Church

Dottie finds that, "The publications of Unity Village, Missouri, prove to be an ever-present help in my quest. They are an organization devoid of dogma but supportive of my inherited social milieu, Christianity. . . . But I will be constrained forever from joining any group in a Sunday-morning get-together. It's a full-blown phobia—my throat constricts, I break out in a sweat, I look furtively for the exit; the whole thing becomes a bust as my thoughts converge on one thing—how do I get out of here! So 'religion' for me consists of Henry David Thoreau . . . and Unity's *Daily Word*. Sufficient for my every need!" She adds, "I've been able to develop a satisfactory concept of 'God' without the machinations of an intermediary. *Never* is there the least temptation to return to the scene of my forty-year bout (encompassing all of my youth) to the Catholic church, or to ever again turn over the reins of my life to someone else. Yes, a happy ending—or beginning."

One woman says she "will continue to live and do as I have been for the last twenty-five years, going [to church only] when I must—weddings, funerals, etc." Another believes "all churches are as bad as the Catholic church. I communicate with God privately on a daily basis. . . . My private prayers with God work best for me." A third, more cynically, says, "Religion is a sham answer to emotional needs and questions. . . . I can't really supply you with a 'happy ending.' Leaving the church has had both advantages and disadvantages. Now, as a convinced atheist I would never really go back. I could not even if I wanted to. . . . I wish there were more atheists. I wish I didn't always have to wonder how 'spirituality' and my lack thereof will affect my relationships."

Kathleen asks, "Can there be a 'happy ending' with an inflexible, unmoving church? I bristle every time I read about the pope telling people in Third World countries to procreate because it is 'God's will.' That comment assumes that God is malevolent and wants people to live in poverty and squalor! My 'personal God' is benevolent." Kathleen's wounds are still fresh. "I do not attend church, but I can't bring myself to explore joining other churches—thirty-three years of being Catholic is not easily cast aside."

Both Inside and Out

Since their initial responses to the survey, a few of the women find themselves straddling a line between being outside of the Catholic church, exploring other denominations, and being an active Catholic once again.

Joan has been attending Unity Church of Christianity. "I am confused and slowly sorting out many aspects of my life. . . . The more I participate at Unity, the more I miss of the Catholic church, so my parents' hopes for my return to Catholicism may well come true."

For Evelyn, church was not important to her for a time. "Then in 1984, my husband and I began to seriously consider having a family. So much of my childhood had been the church and so I was drawn back. The same nagging questions are still there." She apparently has not resolved her doubts.

Ronnie says, "While I have left the church for the most part (I still go on occasion), I have left with a strong sense of spirituality, centeredness, and a sense of social responsibility. From my base of Catholicism, I have learned how we are all part of a whole, and we therefore must work for the whole. I have learned my part in the large scheme of things is to make my corner of the world as best as it can be. I make a difference in the lives of people through my profession as a marriage, family, and child therapist, and through my involvement in various charities. Jesus' model was not to attempt to change the entire world, although in fact he did. His model was to do the best he could where he was at any particular moment. While I credit my parents for instilling this sense of social responsibility, I also credit the church with being a significant contributing factor.

"I also leave the church with an appreciation of the importance of ritual. . . . Rituals bring closure and a sense of peacefulness many times. . . .

"Finally . . . just as I took what my parents could offer and kept some parts, and discarded other parts, I have done so with the church. I have been given a strong foundation to go out into the world. The church has given me the tools I need to live my life as a spiritual, responsible person. How I use those tools is my choice, and I'm sure the guidance will lead me to use them to make the world a better place."

Harriet has one foot in each world: "I enjoy my Unitarian friends on most Sunday mornings and spend Christmas, Easter, and occasional quiet early morning hours in Holy Ghost Church. I consider that I have the best of both worlds though I have to go to two radically different places to get it. Of course I would like the good stuff from both places to be available in one, but that's not realistic."

May tells us of her return since she first answered the survey. She went back to the Catholic church because that is what she knew. "Years went by and I just stayed away from any organized religion. If I wasn't going to be Catholic I wasn't going to be anything else either. I was not interested in joining a church just for the hell of it. I wanted to be a part of it. I would wander into a downtown . . . cathedral for noon mass sometimes, but didn't go to communion. I hadn't been to 'confession' in many years.

"When I moved to San Antonio . . . I was working a few blocks from a downtown church . . . and began going to the noon mass there. . . .

"Well, I became involved in church. It serves the elderly, street people, street teens, and most of all—me. This parish doesn't judge you. You are who you are and are accepted that way. They also have a mass for [the gay group] Dignity on Sunday evening. To me this parish is doing what Christ said to do. They are living the faith! I was commissioned a eucharistic minister . . . and was a minister for the pope's mass when he was here in San Antonio. *Wow!* . . .

"I have come almost full circle to the child I was in the '50s, though not believing as blindly as I once did. I feel comfortable back in the Catholic church, at least in the parish I'm in now.

It is a special place, with special people. I hope I can always find such a welcome place." She ends with: "I no longer have anger or guilt. I know I have a good heart and do try very hard to live a good life, full of God's love. I know that my god will show justice and mercy on me when my time comes to face Him. My God is very loving and knows I'm trying!" She adds, "I am on the inside and outside at the same time."

Conclusion

Chris, the young woman who is quoted throughout this book, wrote to me last summer. She was distraught because she and her fiancé, whom she says are both agnostics, could not have the non-Catholic wedding ceremony they wanted. "My mother was supportive, initially, until we set a date. Suddenly the priest was called, the church was booked, and my freedom as an adult completely disregarded." There was an argument, and Chris was cowed into surrendering. "The worst still lies ahead because we have to sign that ridiculous paper about raising Catholic children. . . . My last consolation now is that after August 22, I will *finally* sever my ties with Catholicism forever." Then she asks for my comments about how she might deal with her situation.

After congratulating her on her upcoming joyous day, I suggested to her that she should just let go of her resentment, otherwise it would control her and ruin her good time at her wedding. I gave her a few other tips. But I focused more on her last comment: "I will *finally* sever my ties with Catholicism forever."

I'll paraphrase my answer to her here. "Ah, if only that could be true! Forgetting that 'Catholic shrapnel' is impossible: it keeps working its way out of your system, at times when you least expect it. And sometimes it's painful. If one of your parents dies, and there is a Catholic funeral mass, will you refuse to receive communion? If a dear friend, a Catholic, asks you to be a god-mother to her baby, will you say no? And if you become a mother-to-be, the expectations will be there for the christening at the church, the first communion, CCD, and so on. What will you do? Only you and your heart can deal with these things as they happen." I went on to advise her that she speak to her parents about her beliefs at some unemotional point, not on Christmas morning or Good Friday or if she were about to give birth.

Becoming an ex-Catholic is at first a conscious, proactive parting with the church. Then it becomes more internalized. Anger subsides when you find a way to feel good about your past, present, and future, as it did with many of the women here when they found peace through therapy and/or a different way of worship.

Then that separation sinks in to deeper levels. For example, you realize you've just walked by a priest and felt no guilt. Or you pass a Catholic church and do not feel anger.

Your past Catholicism will remain with you as a molding force, much like the traditions of your nationality or ethnicity. As a few of the women here have done, you can say "thank you" for that experience. Your future religion is a choice that is with you now, as an adult.

I had a meeting recently in an old building on a Catholic college campus. The people I was to meet with were late, so I wandered around in the stately building, enjoying the turn-of-the-century architectural detail. I went around a corner toward an open door and stepped in. I found myself in a chapel as big as many churches. There was the crucifix, the lit altar candle, the statues, and the heavy smell of wax and incense. I realized I was *appreciating* it all—the symmetry of the altar, the beauty of the candle holders. But I felt no fear. No anger. No guilt. No yearning. I found myself thinking, with great peace, "This is for other people, but it is not for me. I am glad for them. And I am happy for me."

Yes, the Catholic church still does make me angry, when, for example, through its lobbyists it continues to impose its will on society, as it is in central and eastern Europe in its relentless efforts to influence the new governments there to outlaw and criminalize abortion. I still see its dictates taking their greatest toll on women worldwide. At those moments when I wondered if this book was worth writing, that frustration kept me going.

It is women who will change Catholicism and other patriarchal religions, either by leaving them to form their own, or by staying and changing them from within. Getting women to begin to question their own misery is the first step toward this freedom. Getting women to explore their spirituality as they see it—not as it is taught to them—is the next. And perhaps this is the next stage of feminism: a breaking through, or a breaking out, of old molds of worship; abandoning the male-only approach, East and West, for a "whole God"—male and female—approach.

It is my belief that our world is changed by "ordinary people": people like you, like the women here, those who go to work, stand in line at the grocery checkouts, take care of their families. Whether the change you make is to become active again in the Catholic church, and you are happy with that decision, or, if the change you make is for you to leave the Catholic faith, and you are happy with that decision, your journey can be summarized by Jennifer, who wrote this Affirmation:

> We have traveled here this morning over many winding roads. I don't mean literal roads, but liferoads. The twists of fate, and choice, and experience, which have lead us to this place.

Each of us has a story to tell about our journey here. My own road began in a faraway church filled with incense and ceremony. There, in the light of flickering candles, kneeling straight, not daring the luxury of resting my back against the pew, I chanted litanies to saints little-known and long dead. In those days, I conjured up a . . . small, petty god [who] was to haunt me along my journey for many years to come.

I have traveled quite a distance from that faraway church. Yet despite my long-delayed arrival here, I know I've always [belonged here]. . . . Deep down, where what I am today and what I yet may be has always existed, there was a spirit, looking not for freedom *from* religion, but freedom *for* religion. It required only the jolts, abrasions, and general polishing action of life to make it emerge at last.

Epilogue

A friend asked me if "my story" was part of this book. I said to him, "Bits and pieces, yes. But you'll have to read my next book, a novel, to find out the whole thing!" and I laughed.

He pressed on. "No, I mean your story about what you've been through this last year or so. It's all been a test for you, for your faith, and you're doing well with it all. I think you should say something about it."

At first I dismissed his suggestion, thinking it would somehow impose on the material. But after some thinking, I realized it might prove fitting because many things in my life have tried to prevent me from finishing the book, right down to quirky printer problems and software bugs! A long-ago voice in my head would have said, "God's punishing you." But now I tell myself, "It's just another hurdle, just another test, just keep on going on." My faith today has a voice of its own, a comforting one.

And how would that old, recriminating voice explain such events as these: one woman called me three years after seeing a letter of mine to the editor in a newspaper; she called the very evening I was working on chapter 7 and needed one more bit of insight on Women-Church—and she provided it for me. Or the times when I needed a new reference to make a particular point, and there in that day's newspaper was a story that could help me make it. Or when I was thinking that the book would never be published, then I'd hear from one of the women I'd surveyed, out of the blue, asking me how was it going and telling me how important it was that I was writing this book. I consider each of these as gifts that were little treasures.

The year my friend was referring to began in December 1992. I was laid off from my job on a Monday, and on that Thursday learned I absolutely had to have major surgery that I'd been avoiding for months. This would be a hysterectomy because I had several benign fibroid tumors that were contributing to severe anemia.

I had the surgery at the end of February, and as anyone who has had any kind of abdominal surgery will tell you, you are left utterly helpless for several days. My husband of twenty-two years was dedicated in his care of me. I would say it left us both with a new appreciation for one's independence and mortality.

The next bit of news from the doctors, in March, made us appreciate those things even more: it turned out my supposedly benign tumors had been malignant. Malignant! How could this be? There is no cancer in my family, yet they were telling me I'd had lyomyosarcoma. After my husband and I drove home, in silent shock, from the doctor who told me this, we walked into our house, held each other, and wept. We were so fearful.

We had to wait an agonizing two weeks, until April, to see an oncologist, and this was the most trying time. Perhaps the pathologist had misread the slides. Maybe it was really something else. Fibroid tumors are benign 999 times out of 1,000—why did I have to be "the one"? But my faith's voice had a sense of humor ("Why don't I have such luck when it comes to playing the lottery?"), and it finally said, "Why *not* you?" Realizing that I was and am, in the most basic terms, a part of living and dying humanity was somehow comforting: I felt part of the bigger flow of the whole of life, felt part of something bigger than me, which is how I define God.

In that two-week wait, I did what I normally do when I don't understand something: I research. I read everything I could get my hands on, which wasn't much on this type of cancer, so I called every cancer hotline. I was disheartened when I called the National Cancer Institute, based at Dana Farber Cancer Institute in Boston, and the person on the other end of the telephone said, "Malignant fibroids? There is no such thing." But after we spoke, he said he'd send me the latest on what he had, which was more about uterine and endometrial cancer than the type I'd had.

By the time I met with the oncologist, two other pathologists had agreed with the first. But the reassuring news was that this had been caught early, and surgery is the only recommended treatment. Also, recurrence is extremely rare, and although I don't trust the odds in any situation *any* longer, frequent checkups have proven clear. The sense of relief then—and every time my tests come back clear—is incredible. I give my thanks, which for me, takes the form of a silent meditation and a stronger effort to help others around me. As of this writing, I'm fine.

Also in April, I began work as a career counselor for a federally funded agency that specializes in retraining dislocated workers, a job I've loved from the first day. I could drive again, and began running after years of inactivity.

Spring finally came to New England, and then summer. In July, my husband suddenly revealed to me that he had been thinking about living on his own, about being single, about dating other women. He said he didn't understand it all himself, so he couldn't really explain it to me. He said he knew that he'd risk destroying our marriage, something we both treasured, if he left. But he had to answer all these questions.

Mid-life crisis? Male menopause? A reaction to all we'd been through? Even he couldn't explain. After a few painful weeks, he moved out, and he wanted at least six months by himself.

August, September, and October were one sad, dark blur as I descended into a severe depression. I felt like there had been a death, but no funeral. This, surely, was worse than a death—there was no resolution. Every belief I had was being tested. But I never found myself doubting my belief that everything put before us in life has its reason for being there; it is meant to teach us something.

The encouraging words of family and friends carried me through the worst moments. "You have so much to offer," they'd tell me, despite my feeling at the time like I had nothing. Their words kept me going, at times, from hour to hour. They were the cane that provided me with support as I weakly stumbled on.

Being busy with the book, hearing from church members, being busy in general, going to a gym, working many hours, counseling, and attending support groups also helped tremendously. In October, I began attending a separated/divorced support group. I'll never forget, as we went around the circle introducing ourselves that first night, how hard it was for me to say, "I'm separated." After the group was over, I ran to my car, in tears.

But I forced myself to go the next week, and began to see that all of us, whatever our individual situations, shared our pain, and that made it bearable.

The other group I began to attend at about the same time was a hospital-based cancer survivors' support group. This was the first thing I did for myself since my husband left that was not separation-related. It was something I'd been thinking about, and I was finally doing it.

I was early the first evening I attended. I sat quietly as people filed in. One man came in using a walker, another with his wife holding him up. Several women came in with wigs and scarves on. At first, that frightened me because it made me uncomfortable: should I avoid looking at their heads? Will they talk about it?

And what was I doing there, when my cancer appeared to be "over"?

The group shattered my illusions about long-suffering cancer patients. They were *comical*. They were strong. They were not self-pitying. They were, above all, *hopeful*. A few weeks later, when I was telling my oncologist about this, he smiled and said, "That's why I love my job. Cancer patients are the most alive people I know."

The man with the walker was thrilled he could walk upright, however awkwardly, because he'd hated his wheelchair. "I'm making progress," he said of his fight with his brain tumor. "Next, I'll throw this thing away," he said, patting the walker. A woman wearing a wig told those of us new to the group, "A year ago the doctors told me I had an inoperable, untreatable tumor in my hipbone, and to expect only six or more months to live. I'm in chemo off and on, but I'm here, I feel great, and I plan to be around a long time." We applauded. The human spirit was never more alive than in that hospital conference room, with these people.

I was stunned, and moved. And here I thought I'd had problems! Over the next several weeks, I learned from the people in that room how to put things in perspective. Yes, I would have more pain, more roller-coaster ups-and-downs to live through. But now it seemed easier to bear. I could smile again.

And that human spirit in the room? I would call it the presence of the God in each of the people there.

By the fall of 1994, as I write this, I am dating, going to concerts, writing again, and feeling good with the new me-by-myself. My new philosophy is: "Nothing lasts forever. Savor the past, plan for the future, but live in the moment. Life is an adventure that is full of surprises. What doesn't break you makes you stronger. Every day, try something new. Make no excuses."

A large part of my faith says, "Things happen for a reason." Sometimes you don't understand the reason until years later. This became clear to me when lightning hit my house in 1989, setting part of it on fire. My immediate reaction was to be angry that this had happened. It was a major hassle to have to deal with insurance adjusters, to take time away from work to deal with the electrician, the builder, the cleaning people. Worst of all, it made me feel vulnerable in a way I hadn't been before, it made me realize that *anything can happen.* We asked a contractor friend from church to oversee the reconstruction of that part of the house, because his wife had just died and we thought he'd want something to do. He seized the job, working from first light until it was too dark to see anymore. He continued at that pace for weeks.

After it was over, he thanked us. "You saved my sanity by giving me work that kept me busy. Otherwise I would have been sitting home, doing nothing, being depressed. This helped me get through the worst of my grief." So *that* was the reason the house had been hit by lightning: because the work it provided aided our grieving friend. Finally understanding and accepting this gave me much peace.

So while this past year or so has been one of losses, it has been one of found treasures, such as friends who'd had cancer who patiently listened to me express my shock. Others who rallied to support me when Joe moved out. The support groups who showed me how caring new friends could be.

But the whole period has taught me humility and forgiveness, which I'd felt at the Grand Canyon, as well as compassion, true friendship, and love. And best of all, it taught me that those things, those gifts, are within my own heart, where God resides in each of us.

Appendix:
Key to Women in Survey*

Abby
35–40
Psychologist
New Hampshire
Married, 1 child
Irish

Adrianne
24
Teaching assistant
Texas
Single, no children
Nationality unknown

Adele
25
College student advisor
Nebraska
Single, no children
Scandinavian-German-Yugoslav
Mother Lutheran then converted;
    father Catholic

Anita
38
Nanny, writer
Massachusetts
Divorced, 2 children
German-French-English

*Unless specified, parents of each respondent were/are Catholic.

269

Anne
20
Student/tutor
New York
Single, no children
German-Italian-Irish

Annmarie
21
Student
New York
Single, no children
Italian-German-Irish-Russian

Barbara
43
Occupation unknown
Texas
Married, 2 children
Nationality unknown

Bernice
40s
Writer
Connecticut
Married, 1 child
Italian

Beth
45–50
Small business owner
Massachusetts
Divorced, 5 children
Father Irish
Father Catholic, mother converted
    from Episcopalian

Bobbie
30
Post office clerk
New York
Married, no children
German-English
Father Catholic, mother
    Methodist

Candy
36
Military
APO-New York
Single, no children
Canadian

Carmen
age unknown
Occupation unknown
Alaska
Marital status unknown
Nationality unknown

Cassie
49
Store clerk
Louisiana
Divorced, 3 children
French Canadian

Cathy
35
Homemaker
Colorado
Married, 2 children
German-Dutch

Cecile
69
Retired market researcher
California
Married, 7 children
German-Polish-Hungarian
Mother Catholic, father Lutheran

Chris
18
Student
Pennsylvania
Single, no children
Nationality unknown
Father Catholic, mother converted
    from Lutheran

Connie
63
Registered nurse
Florida
Married, 2 children
Irish-Indian-English

Cyndy
26
Entrepreneur/teacher
Pennsylvania
Married, no children
Nationality unknown

Darla
49
Travel agent
California
Married, 3 children
Nationality unknown

Debbie
36
Military administrator
Washington state
Divorced, ? children
Irish-English-German

Diane
46
Company controller
North Carolina
Married, 1 child
Nationality unknown

Donna
25–30
Registered nurse
Minnesota
Married, 1 child
German-Austrian

Dottie
40s
Occupation unknown
California
Marital status unknown
Nationality unknown

Dusty
36
Writer/editor
Pennsylvania
Divorced, 2 children
Polish

Elaine
40s
Antique shop owner
New York
Divorced, 3 children
Spanish

Evelyn
29
Homemaker
South Dakota
Married, 1 child
Norwegian-Welsh-Scot-German
Mother Catholic, father converted
    from ?

Fran
36
Research chemical engineer
Pennsylvania
Divorced, 2 children
Nationality unknown
Father Catholic, mother converted
    from Southern Baptist

Georgia
44
Direct mail specialist
Connecticut
Separated, 1 child
Irish-Scot
Mother Catholic, father's religion
    unknown

Geraldine
65+
Writer/teacher
Washington, D.C.
Widow, 1 child
French Canadian

Ginny
58
Nun/chaplain
Ohio
Single
German-Dutch

Glenna
51
Fiscal coordinator
Pennsylvania
Married, 4 children
English-Italian

Harriet
49
Word processor
Colorado
Single, 2 children
Anglo-Irish

Helen
40
Homemaker
Arizona
Married, 1 child
German-Irish-English

Hillary
30s
Designer
Connecticut
Married, 2 children
Irish-Italian

Holly
39
Educational consultant
Colorado
Married, 2 children
Nationality unknown

Irene
35
Payroll clerk
California
Divorced, no children
Yugoslavian-German

Janet
45
Occupation unknown
Vermont
Divorced, ? children
Nationality unknown

Jeanne
49
Occupation unknown
Colorado
Widow, 2 children
Nationality unknown

Jennifer
45
Writer
Missouri
Married, no children
Nationality unknown

Jill
30
Counselor
New Jersey
Single, no children
Spanish-Irish

Jimi
38
Library clerk
California
Single, no children
Scot-Irish-Austrian
Father Catholic, mother converted
     from ?

Joan
35
Computer operator
Ohio
Divorced, 2 children
German-Irish-Swedish

Judy
48
Office supervisor
Colorado
Marital status unknown, 5
     children
Irish-English

Karen
Age unknown
Occupation unknown
Pennsylvania
Marital status unknown
Nationality unknown

Kathleen
36
High school teacher
Ohio
Single, 1 child
Czech-German

Katrina
40
Traffic clerk
Illinois
Divorced, 1 child
Polish

Kaye
Age unknown
Occupation unknown
California
Marital status unknown
Irish father, Jewish mother

Kelly
45
Office worker
Illinois
Married, 4 children
Irish-English
Mother Catholic, father's religion
    unknown

Lily
50+
Legal administrator
Missouri
Divorced, 4 children
Norwegian-German-Austrian
Mother Catholic, father Lutheran

Linda
20
Student
Texas
Single, no children
Nationality unknown
Mother Catholic, father converted
    from "missionary Baptist"

Lola
35
Hair stylist
Virginia
Married, no children
Nationality unknown

Loretta
48
Systems analyst
New Hampshire
Divorced, 2 children
French Canadian

Louise
24
Marketing specialist
Massachusetts
Single, no children
English

Maggie
56
Homemaker/artist
South Dakota
Married, 4 children
Nationality unknown

Margo
41
Administrative coordinator
Vermont
Married, 2 children
Italian

Martha
35
Staff assistant
Massachusetts
Single, no children
German
Mother Catholic, father's religion
    unknown

MaryAnn
40s
Teacher
Missouri
Divorced, 3 children
German

Maureen
65–70
Psychiatric nurse
Connecticut
Married, 2 children
Irish
Parents were "semi-lapsed"

May
40–45
Law librarian
Texas
Divorced, 3 children
Irish-Dutch-Welsh

Myra
52
Registered nurse
California
Divorced, 5 children
Hungarian-Norwegian
Mother Catholic, father Lutheran

Nan
45
Shop owner
Minnesota
Married, 4 children
German

Natalie
31
Homemaker
Massachusetts
Married, 3 children
Nationality unknown

Nicole
40
Federal employee
California
Married, no children
Nationality unknown

Nora
44
Occupation unknown
California
Single, 1 child
Nationality unknown
Parents Episcopalian but sent her
    to Catholic school

Patricia
22
Writer/typist
New York
Single, no children
Irish

Paula
31
Waitress
Massachusetts
Married, 2 children
Nationality unknown

Peggy
59
Homemaker/writer
South Dakota
Widowed, 9 children
Irish-German

Phyllis
39
Restaurant owner
Ohio
Separated, 1 child
Scandinavian

Polly
30
Restoration artisan
Massachusetts
Married, no children
Nationality unknown
Mother Catholic, father
    Episcopalian

Ricki
32
Graduate student
Illinois
Married, no children
Italian-English-French-German
Mother Catholic, father's religion
    unknown

Roberta
late 30s
Occupation unknown
New York
Marital status unknown
Nationality unknown

Ronnie
23
Psychotherapist
California
Single, no children
Irish-Italian

Rosalie
31
Salesperson
Oklahoma
Divorced, 1 child
Irish-English

Sara
41
IRS clerk
Texas
Divorced, 3 children
Irish-Scot

Susan
42
Psychologist/therapist
Michigan
Married, 2 children
Nationality unknown

Terry
33
Nurse
Connecticut
Married, no children
Hungarian-Austrian-German

Tillie
45–55
Occupation unknown
Massachusetts
Married, 3 children
Nationality unknown

Tina
38
Caretaker
New York
Single, no children
Irish

Victoria
57
Teacher
New York
Married, no children
Italian
Parents were "nominally"
    Catholic

Wanda
63
teacher
Florida
widowed
Czechoslovakian

Yolanda
35
Economist
Massachusetts
Single
Hispanic

Bibliography

Books

Bishop, Peter, and Michael Darton. *The Encyclopedia of World Faiths* (New York: Facts on File, 1988).

Casarjian, Robin. *Forgiveness: A Bold Choice for a Peaceful Heart* (New York: Bantam, 1992).

Gray, Elizabeth Dodson. *Patriarchy As a Conceptual Trap* (Wellesley, Mass.: Roundtable Press, 1982).

Landis, Benson Y. *World Religions* (New York: Dutton, 1965).

Lerner, Gerda. *The Creation of Patriarchy* (New York: Oxford University Press, 1986).

McGuire, Rev. Michael A. *The New Baltimore Catechism and Mass* (New York: Benziger Brothers, 1953).

Melton, J. Gordon. *The Encyclopedia of American Religions* (Detroit: Gale Research, Inc., 1989).

Ochs, Carol. *Behind the Sex of God* (Boston: Beacon Press, 1977).

Pagels, Elaine. *The Gnostic Gospels* (New York: Vintage, 1981).

Ranke-Heinemann, Uta. *Eunuchs for the Kingdom of Heaven* (New York: Penguin, 1990).

Ruether, Rosemary Radford. *Women-Church: Theology and Practice* (San Francisco: Harper and Row, 1985).

Stone, Merlin. *When God Was a Woman* (New York: Harvest/ HBJ Books, 1976).

Weaver, Mary Jo. *Springs of Water in a Dry Land* (Boston: Beacon Press, 1993).

Periodicals/Newspapers

"Bishop Apologizes for Cartoon," Associated Press story, *Patriot Ledger,* December 15, 1993, p. 6.

Brooke, James. "Families Are Smaller in Brazil Despite Roman Catholic Ties," *New York Times* News Service story, *Patriot Ledger,* September 3, 1994, p. 5.

Butturini, Paula. "Rome's New Clerics: Prospects, Perils," *Boston Globe,* December 7, 1993, p. 2.

"Callers React On Soup Kitchen," Associated Press story, *Boston Globe,* December 29, 1993, p. 53.

Matchan, Linda. "Alleged Victims of Porter Decry Elevation of Priest," *Boston Globe,* March 15, 1993, p. 15.

Muello, Peter. "Maverick Theologian Challenges Vatican," Associated Press story, *Patriot Ledger,* December 31, 1993, p. 30.

Index